Wales from the Air

Patterns of Past and Present

Chris Musson

Skokholm Lighthouse, Pembrokeshire

Royal Commission on the Ancient and Historical Monuments of Wales

Cover: The castle and historic town of Caernarfon

**Royal Commission on the Ancient and
Historical Monuments of Wales,
Crown Building, Plas Crug,
Aberystwyth, SY23 1NJ**

The Royal Commission was established in 1908 to make an inventory of the ancient and historical monuments of Wales and Monmouthshire. It is currently empowered by a Royal Warrant of 1992 to survey, record, publish and maintain a database of ancient, historical and maritime sites and structures, and landscapes in Wales. It is responsible for the National Monuments Record of Wales, which is open daily for public reference, for the supply of information to the Ordnance Survey for mapping purposes, for the co-ordination of archaeological aerial photography in Wales, and for the sponsorship of the regional Sites and Monuments Records.

Layout by Chris Musson
Cover and title page by John Johnston
Printed by D Brown & Sons Limited, Bridgend

ISBN 1-871184-14-2

Contents

'Vertical' and 'oblique' air photography...Flying for air photography...National and regional air photography...How air photography works...Continuing the search...Putting the photographs to work...The impact of air photography...The aerial personality of Wales...Flights into the future

Before the Romans...The shape of Roman rule...Castles in the history of Wales...Village, house and garden...Monastic life...Birth and death of an industry...Patterns of industry...Swansea: a city remakes itself

Pembrokeshire in prehistory...Skomer: an island landscape...The edge of Roman rule...From hermit's cell to bishop's palace...Castles and historic towns...Lost gardens rediscovered...Coastal defences at Milford Haven...Aberystwyth and the mining of lead...A contrast in resorts

Early ritual on the North Wales coast...Hillforts, hutgroups, wandering walls...Roman forts and native homesteads...The castles of North West Wales...Slate quarries, copper mines and brickworks

From Ice Age to the use of bronze...Open and enclosed settlements...What discovery? Whose discovery?...A hillfort and its neighbour...Dark Age graves...Castles of the Welsh and English...Castle into house and garden...Lowland and wetland...Moated homesteads...Industry and mineral extraction...The Brenig archaeological trail

Ritual and burial on the Borderland...The Iron Age on the Borderland...Camps, forts and roads of the Roman army...'All the way from sea to sea'...'The palace in the lake'...Castles of earth and timber...Powis Castle: from timber castle to stately home...Vanishing traces of rural life...Leighton Hall and its model farm

Background picture: Snowfall near the confluence of the Rivers Vyrnwy and Severn

Page numbers for illustrations

Preface

This is the Royal Commission's first published essay in air photography and aerial archaeology. It is unlikely to be the last. An aerial study of the country's industrial heritage is one of several already under consideration. As the size and scope of the Welsh air photo collection grows, and fresh insights are drawn from 'vertical' photographs taken for survey and mapping purposes, new themes will no doubt suggest themselves for presentation. For the moment, the aim is to offer a representative sample from the national and regional archives of 'oblique' air photography - views taken with the deliberate purpose of recording the traces of farmer, craftsman, trader and industrial worker in the rural and urban landscape of Wales.

To an extent, too, the book tells the story of Wales from the earliest farming communities to the Industrial Revolution and beyond. Each regional section, emphasising the topographical and cultural diversity which create the distinctive character of Wales, is set out in broadly chronological order. The 'aerial tour' which makes up most of the book is preceded by a fascinating introduction to the techniques, practice and the first achievements of aerial exploration in Wales.

If the words and pictures convince readers that the aerial perspective has a crucial role to play, along with ground-based techniques, in the understanding of Wales in history and prehistory, it will have met its first objective. If it whets the reader's appetite for future publications, and for further work in air photography and air photo analysis, it will properly reflect the Royal Commission's aim of involving the people of Wales in the exploration, recording and interpretation of the patterns of the past so spectacularly preserved in the landscape and townscape of the present day.

J Beverley Smith
Chairman of Commissioners

At the time of going to press the present counties of Dyfed, Gwynedd, Clwyd, and Powys, along with Gwent and the three counties of Glamorgan - broadly the five 'regions' used in the book - are about to be replaced by unitary authorities, the names and boundaries of which are not yet firmly fixed. For this reason county names are generally avoided in the text, sites being related instead to towns or other landmarks marked on the map of Wales on page 4. Correct Welsh spellings have been used throughout, except in the few cases where this might have created confusion with mapped information or published archaeological texts.

Many of the illustrated sites lie on private land, and cannot be visited without the owners' permission. Some of the rural sites can be viewed from public footpaths. Most of the castles and abbeys are open to the public.

'Oblique' air photography: the village and fields of Templeton, in Pembrokeshire

Air photography and aerial archaeology

The camera is essential to this book, but simply as a tool, a means of capturing images that explore or explain the patterns of the past in the landscape of the present day. The pictures may be striking, and all the more effective for that, but their real value lies in what they say about the mingling of 'then' and 'now' in countryside, village and town. How did fields or streets take on their present form? Can photographs show how the land was used over the centuries? Can we see from the air things that are invisible, or nearly so, from the ground? Can we use air photography to help preserve and manage the landscape, not just of distant history or prehistory, but also of our parents and grandparents?

Photography, in this sense, is only a beginning. But it is also an end, every photograph drawing on the accumulated skills of photographer and pilot, navigating accurately and safely in the air, being in the right place at the right time, judging the play of light and shade, knowing how crops behave, appreciating the special effects of ice and snow, all through an eye and mind sharpened to what is, or might be, there to record below.

It has been suggested, mischievously perhaps, that aerial archaeology is a study in its own right. True, it offers special insights, but then so do excavation, field survey, the study of maps and documents, and the analysis of pottery, bones and pollen. Each also has its limitations, aerial archaeology no less than the rest. If this book has a theme, it is not so much the special character of aerial archaeology as the need for partnership with these sister techniques in our quest for a more rounded picture of the past.

'Vertical' and 'oblique' air photography

Archaeologists use two types of air photography: *oblique* or perspective views like that on the left, and *vertical* photography, shown at upper right. Vertical photography is taken with sophisticated cameras from specially modified aircraft, mainly for survey and mapping purposes. It is expensive, and archaeologists can rarely afford to commission it for their own purposes. They therefore draw on the vast collections of photographs in existing archives, perhaps three million frames already for Wales, with more accumulating each year. Oblique photographs, by contrast, are generally taken by the archaeologists themselves, from the open window of a two-seater or four-seater light aircraft, hired from a local airfield. The cameras and films are quite simple - there is a short note on page 156 for those interested in such things.

While vertical photography records the whole of the landscape, oblique photography covers only what the photographer sees and judges to be significant. What he fails to see, or understand, he inevitably fails to record. Vertical photography therefore has a special value in study of the whole landscape, or of settlements in their broader context. Oblique photography is unrivalled in recording individual sites or areas of historic interest, the more so because the photographer can choose the time of day or year, and the kind of lighting, that will show walls or earthworks to the best advantage.

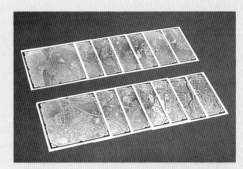

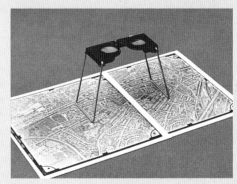

'Vertical' air photographs and portable stereoscope
Top. *Two runs of overlapping vertical photographs.* Below. *Two prints set up for three-dimensional viewing through a portable stereoscope. Both the physical character and the topographical setting of archaeological features are better seen in three dimensions than in individual two-dimensional photographs. More sophisticated stereoscopes allow larger areas to be viewed and accurate measurements to be made. Expensive computerized photogrammetric plotters can be used to make detailed contoured plans from such photographs, to an accuracy of as little as ten centimetres.*

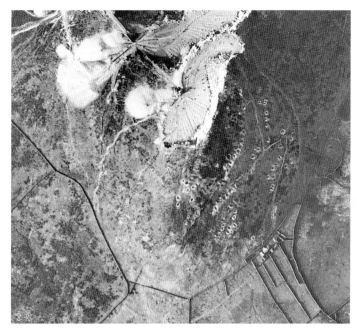

Early air photograph of Braich y Dinas hillfort, Penmaenmawr
Air photography has a long history, starting (by balloon) over Paris in the 1850s, reaching Britain by the first decade of the twentieth century, and being used for intelligence work in both World Wars. The archaeological use of air photography from powered aircraft began in the 1920s, notably with pioneering photography of known and newly discovered sites in southern England.

The photograph shown here is one of the earliest from Wales, taken on a sortie by the No5 Flying Training School of the Royal Air Force on 26 September 1923. A near-vertical view, it shows hut-circles under excavation in the Iron Age (and perhaps later) hillfort of Braich y Dinas, on the North Wales coast west of Conwy. The quarrying seen encroaching on the hillfort at the top of the picture has now totally destroyed the hilltop on which it once stood.

High-wing aircraft for air photography
The high wing leaves a clear view downward for the photographer, who works through an opening window from his seat alongside the pilot. Here, the aircraft is a four-seater Cessna 172, which can carry a second archaeologist or navigator if need be. In the background is a low-wing aircraft, less suitable for air photography because of its more limited view of the countryside below.

Vertical photographs do, of course, contain archaeological information, but more by accident than design, and for the most part they are taken at times that suit mapping rather than archaeological recording. In their professional work archaeologists use the two types more or less equally, but in this book it is the oblique view that predominates, if only for its fresh perspective on aspects of the landscape that may appear quite different from ground level.

Flying for air photography

The effectiveness of oblique air photography depends on the archaeologist's capacity to take to the air, often at short notice, in the right conditions of lighting or crop development and in the chosen target area.

In general there is free access to the air over most of Britain, apart from control zones around airfields, and forbidden areas over military ranges (though most of these are open at weekends or in the evening).

Apart from this, and with due respect for air safety and aircraft maintenance, the archaeologist needs no one's permission to fly, or to take photographs of anything that seems to be of historical interest. By and large, no one has to approve the photographs, as is required in many other countries, so they can be made readily and quickly available through publicly accessible photo-libraries.

In practice, the greatest problems are usually the uncertainty of the weather and the difficulty of arranging simultaneous availability of aircraft, pilot and photographer - there may be only a few hours' notice of good sunshine or clear visibility, and any of the participants may by then be committed to other things, especially in locally based air survey, where most of the people concerned have overriding responsibilities in conservation or rescue archaeology.

Once in the air the photographer has to work quickly and efficiently, and to note details of the flight path and targets so that the photographs can be rapidly catalogued afterwards. This means careful planning of flights so that the search areas, and existing information about them, are fresh in the photographer's mind. Sometimes, if the targets are known sites, a flight path can be planned in soft pencil on 1:50000 ('1-inch') Ordnance Survey maps. At other times the object may be exploratory work on a previously unsurveyed piece of upland, or the search for 'new' sites in an area that has produced others in the past.

Inevitably, many flights do not go as planned: cloud may cover the survey area, or the anticipated 'new' sites may simply not appear. If the photographer has only one type of target in view, reverses of this kind can prove very wasteful; a flight abandoned half-way through will still have taken several hours of planning, travel, and camera preparation, along with valuable air time, and hence money (a suitable aircraft may cost between £60 and £160 an hour to hire). Archaeologists therefore try to work to a broader 'portfolio' of targets, any of which can be called into play if a flight has to depart from its original plan.

Flights may be as short as thirty minutes, or as long as three hours or more, the normal endurance of a light aircraft with full fuel tanks. In the air, the pilot and archaeologist work as a team, relying closely on one another. The pilot concentrates on putting the aircraft in the right place, and on matters such as safety, the weather, fuel checks and radio contact with ground control. The archaeologist identifies targets, including the next but one whenever possible, and gives detailed instructions about the flight path, using voice or hand-signals. He also operates two or three cameras (for black-and-white and perhaps two types of colour film), and records the flight path by one of several methods (marks on the flying map, tape recorder, notes on a knee pad, or simply trained memory).

Once the flight is over, the process continues with the immediate writing of a flight report, the rapid processing of the films, and the cataloguing of the results. Every photograph must be numbered, located on the map, and indexed so that both it and its subject matter (Roman fort, native settlement, landscape view, or whatever) can be readily retrieved from the library shelves or slide collection. In much of this work pen and paper have now given way to computers, so that information can be quickly recalled or re-ordered if need be.

National and regional air photography

Like the rest of Britain, Wales has both national and regional flying programmes. The national programme is carried out by the Royal Commission, the regional programmes by the four Archaeological Trusts which deal with conservation and rescue archaeology in Wales. The Trusts cover, respectively, south-east, south-west, north-west, and north-east and central Wales. Cambridge University also carried out oblique photography over Wales from the end of World War II until 1981, but since then the university has concentrated on vertical photography, not always for archaeological purposes.

The strength of regional air survey is that it is done by people with an intimate knowledge of the local landscape and archaeology, and of the questions that might be answered through air photography. The merit of national survey is that it can range over the whole country, concentrating on areas or types of recording not adequately covered by the regional fliers. Co-ordination of objectives and coverage is not a problem since both programmes are funded by the Royal Commission. At the time of writing, the total air time in Wales amounts to about 100 hours a year, covering around 1700 'locations', including about 600 scheduled ancient monuments and perhaps 300-400 sites new to the archaeological record.

Inevitably there is pressure for more to be done, if only because the technique is so cost effective across the entire range of exploration, recording and heritage management. Nonetheless, much has been achieved on present resources, as the pictures in this book show. The priority in the coming years will probably be for more work on the analysis of existing photographs, both vertical and oblique, so that the information they contain can be added to the mapped and written records of the Royal Commission and other heritage bodies in Wales.

Earthwork enclosures at Gaer Du, Llandrindod Wells
These two views show the effect that lighting and camera angle can have on the recording of slight earthworks. In the top picture the oval enclosure on the right is picked out well by low cross-lighting, but little else is visible. In the lower view, with the sun from a different angle, the rectilinear enclosure in the background becomes equally clear through the highlights and shadows of its low banks. This second enclosure was first discovered from the air, and is barely detectable on the ground. If the sun were high or the skies cloudy, giving only short shadows or none at all, even the most perceptive air photographer would find it difficult to make out the lesser enclosure.

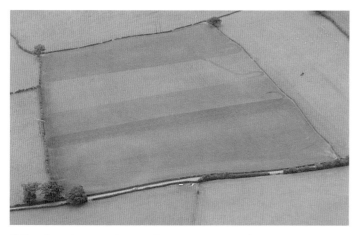

Soilmarks and cropmarks at Dyffryn Lane, near Welshpool
A Neolithic 'henge', or ritual enclosure, and two Bronze Age round barrows on the central Borderland, first discovered from the air. In the soilmark view (above) the mounds of the barrows and the external bank of the henge appear as lighter marks where the plough has cut into the upcast subsoil used in their construction. In the cropmark view (below) the ditch and entrance causeway of the henge occupy the foreground, with the ring-ditches of the smaller barrows beyond. A 'blob' on the far right may mark a pit or ritual shaft, and there are also the lines of an early field system.

How air photography works

Air photographers exploit five main phenomena in their work:
* the high viewpoint;
* the effect of light and shade;
* differences in the colour of the soil;
* variations in the colouring of crops and vegetation;
* special conditions created by frost, snow, ice and flood.

The high viewpoint enjoyed from around 300-400 metres, the normal height for oblique air photography, allows wide-spreading patterns to be seen as a whole rather than in separate parts, and gives coherence to complex or partly destroyed features which are virtually unintelligible from ground level. The landscape view on the Contents page and the picture of Templeton on page 8 are good examples.

Shadow and highlight are used to emphasize physical features which may be almost invisible on the ground - the barely detectable earthworks of prehistoric fields, for instance, or the heavily eroded defences of a Roman fort. Aerial archaeologists therefore make the most of early-morning or late-evening sun, and the low sunshine of the winter months. Winter opportunities tend to be few in Britain, however, perhaps a score of days between October and March, at the most. Low-light or shadow photography is particularly effective in upland areas, where there has been less erosion by modern ploughing; but it can also be productive in lowland areas, throwing patterns of 'humps and bumps' into relief by the play of light and shade.

Soilmarks appear as changes of colour, texture or dampness in ploughed fields before the growth of the crops obscures the bare soil. The difficulty, for the aerial archaeologist, is to arrive over the fields at the right time, when the soil is damp and fresh from the plough or harrow. In a sparsely ploughed country like Wales this is doubly difficult, and soilmarks have not yet been recorded in any number.

Cropmarks provide archaeologists with one of their most striking tools of discovery, the sites revealed rarely being detectable by any other means. Cropmarks appear as differences of height or colour in crops which are under stress, usually through lack of water or some other nutrient. This is most likely to occur in light and well-drained soils,

Cropmarks can sometimes be seen from the ground, though they are rarely intelligible from this level. Here, the green cropmark above the ditch of the Dyffryn Lane henge can be clearly seen and undertood. From the same viewpoint, however, all the other cropmarks in the field were invisible. Cropmarks seen from ground level or from nearby hills have been reported by writers from the seventeenth century onwards.

'Negative' cropmarks above buried walls at Caerwent Roman town

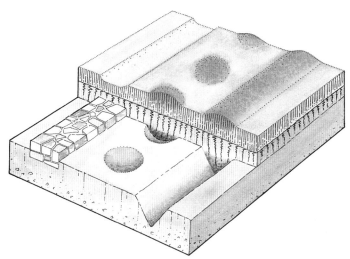

The formation of cropmarks
Crops grow taller and ripen later over the deeper, more nutritious and damper soil of a buried ditch or large pit. Growth is stunted and the ripening of the crop earlier in shallower soil above buried walls or other impervious deposits. Ditches and pits create green marks in the yellowing crop ('positive' cropmarks). Walls and the like give yellow marks in the green crop ('negative' cropmarks). Both can persist as 'yellow-on-yellow' marks in the ripened crop. (After a drawing by B Bennison for the Clwyd-Powys Archaeological Trust.)

above soft and permeable rocks or gravels; as a result, the distribution across the countryside is uneven.

Cropmarks appear most frequently in ripening grain, between mid-June and early August, especially when the weather has been dry at critical stages of growth or ripening. In wetter years the crops may never come under enough stress to develop cropmarks, even where they have been regularly seen in the past. Cropmarks sometimes appear at other times of year - in March or April in germinating crops, in the spectacular yellow flowers of oil seed rape in May, or in pulses and root crops such as sugar beet as late as September or October.

In times of extreme drought grassland, too, can produce remarkably clear cropmarks, or 'parchmarks', the green of the still-growing grass contrasting starkly with the bleached brown of the parched pasture alongside. This happens, for the most part, for only a few days two years in ten, whereas cropmarks in grain can be seen at various times throughout a period of six to eight weeks almost every other year.

Cropmark enclosure at Glancleddau, near Llawhaden
This cropmark enclosure closely resembles the one shown on page 55, and lies only a kilometre from it. The pictures on the left, taken within a few seconds of one another in 1990, show how the angle of view sometimes influences the clarity with which the cropmark is rendered. The third picture, taken two years later, shows the need for repeated visits: the uphill circuit of the enclosure's outer ditch, not showing as a cropmark on the earlier flight, is now detectable in the right-hand fields, while the rest of the settlement is virtually invisible.

Grass-parching is therefore highly prized by aerial archaeologists, since it extends the impact of cropmark photography to areas dominated by pasture rather than by arable cultivation.

In general, cropmarks reveal only major ditches or buried features, a metre or more across and at least half that in depth. Lesser gullies or fence lines are unlikely to be seen, and if an ancient farmstead, or archaeological feature of any other kind, has created little ground disturbance it will not normally reveal itself through cropmark photography. Buried roads and wall foundations can sometimes be seen, as in the Roman town of Caerwent (top right); on occasion even the layout of long abandoned flower beds can be revealed (page 14).

Frost, snow, ice and flood offer special opportunities, though airfields or pilots may be difficult to reach at such times. Snow suppresses distracting colour and gives excellent conditions for low-light photography; wind-blown snow can also show up changes of level that are barely visible under normal conditions, as in the background picture on the Contents page. The melting of frost by sun or wind, or the persistence of ice at the end of a cold spell, may also reveal otherwise unsuspected buried features. Flooding, too, may show up old river courses and explain the location of roads or farmsteads in a way that could otherwise be achieved only by painstaking survey on the ground.

Continuing the search

All of these techniques rely to an extent on the luck of the moment, or on factors beyond human control. Barley, wheat and oats, for instance, ripen at different times between June and August, demanding repeated flights, at intervals of a few days, to catch each crop at its critical stage. The same applies from year to year. A settlement that is barely visible one year may twelve months later be as clear as if it had been 'painted' on the field, and then not be seen again for a decade. Along the central Welsh Borderland, now fairly well explored from the air, about four out of every ten cropmarks photographed are new to the record (taken over a three-year cycle), while even the most intensively surveyed parts of England still produce worthwhile discoveries, especially in years of drought.

The same may be said of low-light photography, which in most areas of the country will continue to produce new information as the light strikes differently on each new flight. In addition, new aspects of the historic landscape come into focus as the years go by; industrial archaeology, for example, has only recently become the subject of intensive aerial work, as has the recording of present-day features before redevelopment.

The effective recording of the historic landscape therefore requires repeated visits, preferably by local archaeologists or experienced 'national' fliers, at different times of the day and year, and for many years in succession. Even then, it will be decades rather than years before we can be confident that a representative sample, let alone the whole, of the available evidence has been collected for most parts of the country.

A 'lost' garden layout at Gregynog, near Newtown
Alongside the imitation half-timbering of the Davies's mansion, now the University of Wales study and conference centre, summer parching picks out earlier flower beds in the level surface of the present-day lawn.

The River Vyrnwy in flood, near Welshpool
Flooding offers special opportunities to record the detailed topography of river valleys and other low-lying areas.

Snow photography in central Wales

Left. Melting of a light snowfall reveals the ditches of a previously unknown hilltop enclosure in the hills south of the Tanat Valley. Shadows show that parts of the banks and ditches still survive as earthworks.

Right. Some years later the hillfort shows as crop-marks in the parched grass of a summer drought.

Below. On upland pasture south-west of Corwen modern walls and fences overlie the narrower strips of an earlier field system, barely detectable on the ground and perhaps medieval or post-medieval in date. The diffuse earthworks are emphasized by low winter sunlight and a thin cover of wind-blown snow, which suppresses distracting colour variations in the midwinter undergrowth. First identified from the air, the field system could also be mapped with reasonable accuracy from the air photographs.

Putting the photographs to work

One of the merits of aerial survey is that the information, ideas and photographs that it produces can be turned to practical use in many aspects of research and conservation, preferably in conjunction with other approaches such as documentary research and excavation. Inevitably, the various uses overlap and merge with one another.

Illustration and record

Because of their high viewpoint, aerial photographs (whether vertical or oblique) provide an objective and intelligible record of the whole or large parts of an archaeological site or complex, only portions of which are visible from any single point on the ground. The quality of the record will vary with the direction of view, the lighting and local crop development and, in oblique photography at least, with the skill and perceptiveness of the photographer.

However, the record is not complete. It cannot, in most cases, reveal the date or function of the features recorded, except by comparison with similar features already explored and dated elsewhere. But the photograph does provide an objective record: it cannot of itself contain any human bias of description, representation or interpretation, as may be so with a drawn plan or map in which the surveyor has had to decide what to draw and what to omit. The photograph can, of course, have bias projected upon it at a later stage, during interpretation or mapping for comparison with information from other sources, including other air photographs.

In addition to creating an objective record, skilfully taken oblique air photographs can record, and thus describe or illustrate, individual sites or landscapes with great clarity and subtlety. The photographs in this book will show how powerful the technique can be in describing not only the site itself but also its topographical setting, whether in an urban or a rural context.

Discovery and illustration: Graig Fach-goch, near Tywyn
A previously unrecorded enclosure, probably a pre-Roman hillfort, seen at the moment of its discovery from the air. In places the enclosing bank underlies the modern field walls but elsewhere it diverges to create a curving enclosure with an apparent entrance gap on the far side. Air photographs of this kind are valuable in illustrating the landscape setting of sites, here looking across upland pasture to the long shoreline of Cardigan Bay, on the western coast of Wales.

Interpretation: Offa's Dyke, near Montgomery
Here, the ridge and furrow field system at lower right raised important questions of dating and interpretation, since the earthwork which crosses the lower part of the picture is the eighth-century Offa's Dyke. Could the apparent alignment of the ridges on either side of the Dyke mean that the fields were earlier? Intensive ground survey suggested otherwise but, if confirmed, the interpretation would have been an important one. Air survey can raise such possibilities; ground survey or excavation is usually needed to prove or disprove them.

Interpretation

The wide coverage of the aerial viewpoint can help archaeologists to interpret or re-interpret complicated sites and landscapes. Continuities or contrasts between the different parts of a pattern often become clear, and ideas may be generated for testing against other photographs, or against ground-based observation or excavation. Follow-up surveys on the ground are always desirable, if only to note the general character of the site and its setting. Air photographs rarely tell the whole story, and great care is needed in using them as the sole source of information, especially where the pattern is at all complex, either internally or in its relationship to the local topography, land use or vegetation.

Discovery

The most dramatic use of air photography lies in the discovery of 'new' sites or landscapes, or of new information about those already known to archaeologists. Sometimes the same features are actually visible from ground level, but have escaped recognition until seen from the all-embracing aerial viewpoint. This may be so with low banks, ditches, and field divisions, or with stone walls and foundations which have become half-obscured by erosion or plant growth. In other cases, aerial survey may be the only realistic means of discovery, though even cropmark or soilmark sites can sometimes be seen - though not readily understood - from ground level (see page 12, for instance).

The important point is that the aerial perspective, and the capacity of the air photographer to recognize the significance of the recorded information, provide rapid and wide-ranging means of identifying and recording man-made features not yet known to archaeologists. The impact of such discoveries can be revelatory, as shown by the two examples on page 19.

Mapping

Archaeological air photographs are produced in great numbers - perhaps 50,000 oblique images each year in Britain, along with a far larger number of vertical photographs taken for survey or monitoring purposes. These photographs remain on file or on public access as primary records, and should be consulted directly if certain kinds of questions are to be answered. For most uses, however, their content is best communicated through drawn plans, maps and written or codified descriptions, bringing together observations from many photographs in documents or computer records similar to those used to summarize the results of other kinds of archaeological work, such as ground survey. The conversion of thousands of photographs into a more usable number of lists, descriptions and drawings is the first step in putting the photographs to work, whether in conservation or research.

For cropmarks and soilmarks, mapping from air photographs is the only way of achieving this transition. For low earthworks or wider areas of preserved landscape, transcription from photographs may be the most economical means of achieving an initial record, for later improvement and modification by ground survey if resources allow. The methods used are described briefly on page 18.

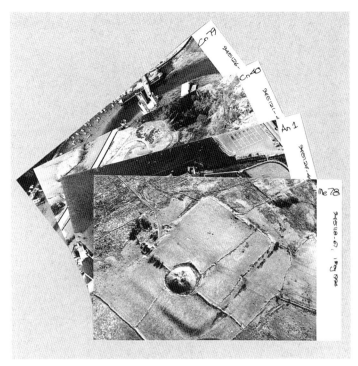

Conservation: aerial monitoring of scheduled ancient monuments
Some of the photographs from the programme of regular aerial monitoring that helps Cadw:Welsh Historic Monuments to care for the most valued field monuments of the country of Wales.

Conservation

Anything which creates a better appreciation of the historic landscape also helps indirectly in its preservation. Air photographs often have a dramatic effect in emphasizing the importance of individual sites and landscapes, and they are widely used by archaeologists with this in mind. At a more immediate level, the rapid inclusion of aerial discoveries in national and local records can influence local authority policies and individual planning decisions.

A particularly direct application in conservation work was pioneered in the 1980s by Cadw:Welsh Historic Monuments, and the programme is now continued by the Royal Commission and the regional Archaeological Trusts. This involves the regular monitoring from the air of the country's 2700 scheduled ancient monuments, those designated by the Secretary of State as particularly worthy of preservation in the national context. Around a quarter are photographed each year, on a rolling programme that provides total coverage every four or five years. The photographs are used not only to detect damage, or the risk of damage, but also to create a gradually improving aerial record of the country's most important heritage sites, invaluable to Cadw's ground-based staff when they visit owners and tenants to discuss the sympathetic management and protection of the sites for future enjoyment and research.

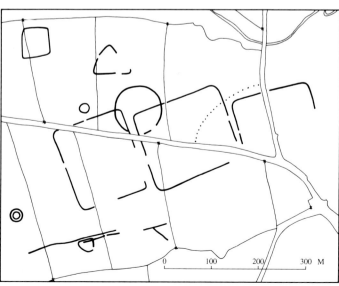

Mapping from air photographs: cropmarks at Walton, near New Radnor
The picture shows three Roman practice camps and other cropmarks on the central Borderland. Mapping (or 'transcription') is done by matching the archaeological information on the photograph against the known positions of field boundaries, roadlines and similar features on existing maps. The accuracy of the transcription will depend on the accuracy of the maps and on the photo-interpreter's capacity to identify already-mapped 'control points' on the photograph. The control-points used in the transcription on the left, made from this and other photographs, have been marked by asterisks on the resulting drawing.

Sketch-plotting, or plotting 'by eye', can place most archaeological features within about five metres of their true position, good enough for most uses in planning and conservation. Plotting a cropmark complex like the one shown above might take an experienced photo-interpreter about half an hour.
Computer-aided transcription, using desktop computers and custom-made programs, can be accurate to two metres or less, but will take two or three times as long, especially when separate plots are made from a number of photographs, as may be required in difficult terrain or for complex sites.
Photogrammetric plotting, using vertical photographs and much more expensive equipment, is capable of producing fully contoured plans, accurate to within ten centimetres, but may require a whole day for such a site.

The impact of air photography

The Roman army in Wales

Wales, like other parts of Britain, has a fair number of Roman military sites, still visible above the ground, or brought to light through the discovery of Roman material during ploughing or building work. From the late 1940s, until about 1980, an aerial search for Roman military sites was carried out over Wales and the Borderland, whenever the opportunity arose, by the late Professor J K S St Joseph of Cambridge University, and by his colleague and eventual successor, David Wilson. Previously unrecorded forts and temporary camps, along with roads, practice works and civil settlements, were reported in a steady stream over the years, so that by 1980 the map of Roman military Wales (right, with some recent additions) consisted in some areas mainly of 'air photo' sites. Without these any attempt at rational explanation of the pattern of Roman military establishments in Wales would be impractical, or at least unreliable.

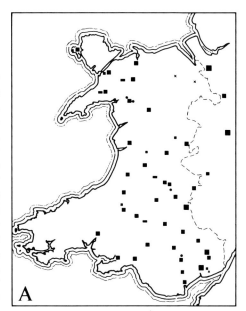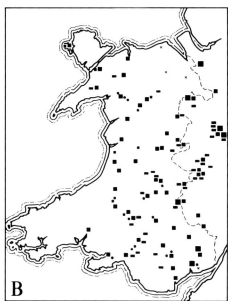

Roman military sites in Wales and the Borderland
A: *without aerial evidence.* **B:** *with aerial evidence.*
Squares of decreasing size represent fortresses, forts and fortlets. Rectangles are temporary camps, and circles practice works. Uncertain sites are marked by crosses.

Cropmark evidence on the Borderland

When aerial exploration of Shropshire and the central Borderland began soon after World War II there were few known cropmark sites, and even by 1959 (near right) the pattern was mainly restricted to small clusters around the Roman forts at Wroxeter, Montgomery and Caersŵs, reflecting the Cambridge University programme described above. In the 1960s, as private fliers from England joined the search, the sites grew in number and became more evenly scattered across the map. The process accelerated in the 1970s when locally-based air survey began along the Borderland through the work of the Clwyd-Powys Archaeological Trust. By 1979 (far right) the map had been completely transformed, and the pattern of discovery has continued unabated to the present day. The contrast between 1959 and 1979 demonstrates the fundamental contribution that aerial survey can make to the fund of evidence available to archaeologists and landscape historians for their re-creations of the past.

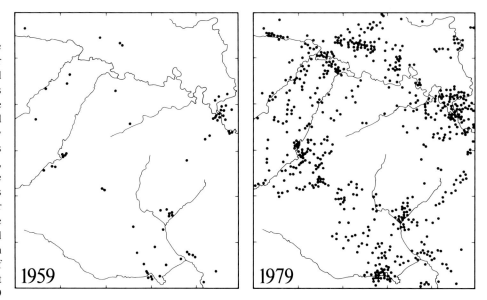

Cropmark sites on the Borderland: discovery, 1959-1979
Cropmark sites of all kinds in an area 60 x 50 kilometres across on the central Borderland. The Border runs down the centre of the frame, with the River Severn towards the top. The cluster of sites at upper right is around Wroxeter and Shrewsbury, and that at centre left around Welshpool and Montgomery.

The aerial personality of Wales

The topographical map of Wales (page 4) shows a deeply indented mountainous spine running the length of the country from north to south. Peninsulas at the west clasp the great sweep of Cardigan Bay. Off the north coast stands the large island of Anglesey, one of the widest-spreading lowland areas in the country. For anyone flying over Wales the dominating impression is of enormous variety in topography and landscape, and equally striking variations in regional archaeology. The topography owes much to a complex underlying geology, but with major contributions from uplift, erosion and glaciation. More recently, the direct impact of man has made the present-day landscape very different from that of 500 or 5000 years ago.

Solid geology

Precambrian rocks, 570 million or more years old, reach the surface on Anglesey and along parts of the north coast, with smaller exposures at the extreme south-west, and across the Border in Shropshire. Volcanic and other hard rocks of the Cambrian and Ordovician series form the mountain peaks of Snowdonia and north-west Wales, along with the Berwyn Range of the northern Borderland and the more heavily eroded Preseli Hills of Pembrokeshire. Succeeding these across central Wales and the northern Borderland are resistant Ordovician rocks, with (to the south-east) more eroded Silurian deposits, the latest accumulating about 400 million years ago. Much of South Wales stands on Devonian sandstones and grits, 400-350 million years old, with an overlying 'oval' of Carboniferous Limestone and Coal Measures, so important to the industrial developments of the past two centuries. In the north-east a band of similar rocks spreads southward from the Dee Estuary to the hills west of Wrexham. These rocks bring the record to about 280 million years ago. Younger sediments of Permian and Triassic origin, 280-190 million years old, underlie the low land of the Cheshire Plain and the Vale of Clwyd at the north-east, and flank the Severn Estuary in the south. Offshore, and in a thin cover across parts of the southern coastal plain, are sedimentary rocks of the early Jurassic, 190-150 million years old. After this Wales remained an upstanding land-mass, with no further rock formation but with major effects from uplift and distortion of the earlier strata.

Landform

The over-riding impression of the central uplands, from the air, is of a wide-spreading plateau or series of plateaux, deeply indented by narrow valleys but with limited areas projecting to higher levels - Cadair Idris in the west, Snowdonia and the peaks behind Harlech in the north-west, the Berwyn Range in the north-east, and the Brecon Beacons and flanking mountains in the south. On the lower ground, too, geologists see evidence of similar plateaux, though they are less obvious from the air. In Glamorgan and Pembrokeshire, for instance,

Glacial landforms at Llyn y Fan Fach, near Llandeilo

21

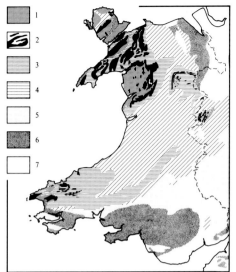
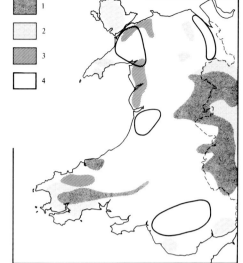

Wales: solid geology
1 Precambrian and Cambrian rocks
2 Igneous/volcanic intrusions and extrusions
3 Ordovician   4 Silurian   5 Devonian
6 Carboniferous 7 Permian, Triassic and Jurassic

Wales: drift geology and surface deposits
Surface deposits vary from glacial boulder clays (1), which rarely produce cropmarks, to more favourable sands and gravels (2). In many areas surface deposits are absent or have not yet been identified (3).

Wales: main results of air photography, to 1994
1 Productive areas for cropmark photography
2 Recent or more scattered cropmark returns
3 Upland areas with good earthwork photography
4 Recent industrial recording by RCAHMW

there are well-defined platforms at about 60 and 120 metres, the second also spreading along much of the Cardigan Bay coast. Another terrace can be seen at around 180 metres, notably in north Pembrokeshire and along the southern part of Cardigan Bay. In the interior there are identifiable plateaux at higher levels.

On both high and low ground, however, these plateaux slice with remarkable indifference across the underlying geology, showing that the basic form of the present-day landscape emerged through a series of pulsed uplifts of the underlying rocks, each followed by a period of erosion which created a temporary landscape of plain and projecting hills, before the process began again at what now appears to us as a 'lower' level. The agency of erosion remains unclear. Some writers favour the gradual unmasking of the upland plateaux from beneath deeply weathered and now vanished rocks by the effects of wind and rain in an open landscape. Others apply to the upper platforms the same processes of marine erosion in a shallow sea that are universally accepted for the lower platforms of the coastal fringe.

Whatever the cause, there is common agreement that the finer details of the current landform derive mainly from the repeated advance and retreat of ice sheets during the last two million years, creating some of the most spectacular glacial landscapes seen anywhere in Britain.

Advance and retreat of the ice

Wales has undergone at least five episodes of almost total ice cover, and much longer intervening stages of sub-arctic conditions, during the last two million years. The latest glaciation, covering all of Wales except parts of Pembrokeshire and the southern seaboard, reached its peak between 21,000 and 16,000 years ago, after which sub-arctic conditions preceded the arrival of a more temperate (but still fluctuating) climate, from about 10,000 years ago.

Working on the landscape of high and low plateaux described above, the ice sheets repeatedly ground and moulded the land surface to typical glacial forms, notably the sweeping *cwms* that once held the heads of glaciers, and the steep-sided and round-bottomed glacial valleys, seen most spectacularly in Snowdonia, with ribbon-lakes where the glaciers once cut deeply into the underlying bedrock.

Equally important are the depositional effects of glaciation and ice-sheet cover. Boulders and stones ripped from the underlying surface, mixed with finely ground particles weathered from the surrounding slopes, have been redeposited as sheets of glacial *till*, often clay and boulders but elsewhere largely of stones and gravel, filling inland valleys or blanketing the lower land of south Wales, the northern Borderland and all except the most mountainous parts of north-west Wales, including the heavily eroded strata of Anglesey.

Many other depositional features associated with glaciation can be seen. The north-eastern town of Wrexham, for instance, sits on a 'fan' of gravel left by the outflow from the edge of the most recent ice-sheet, and to its east there are great arcs of 'terminal' and 'lateral' moraine, respectively the debris dropped at the snout of a glacier and material from the edge of the ice-sheet.

Also prominent, and softening some of the ice-worn profiles of the glacial landscape, are the widespread products of erosion, landslip and soil-creep during the long periods of sub-arctic conditions between the episodes of total or partial glaciation.

Climate

Wales is too small to have a noticeable difference of temperature from south to north, but the mountainous spine creates significant variations between west and east. The prevailing Atlantic weather systems bring moist and relatively warm air from the west and south-west, or less commonly showery and cool polar air from the north-west and north. Less frequently, cold weather in winter and hot weather in summer approach from the east or south-east. In both cases the central mountains obstruct or soften the passage of these systems across Wales, so that - broadly speaking - the west coast has a relatively warm, moist and equable (though windy) climate, while the eastern Borderland is drier and less exposed, with greater seasonal variations of temperature higher in summer and up to 2.5°C lower in winter, compared with the far south-west). Along the south coast the climate is more like that of the Borderland, though warmer in winter and with higher cumulative temperature over the year than any other part of Wales.

Soils, vegetation and land use

Geology, landform and climate (before the 'greenhouse effect' of recent years) remain uninfluenced by man. Soils and vegetation, by contrast, owe much to the use that has been made of the landscape and its natural resources over the past 10,000 years. In the latter part of this period political, social and economic factors also come into play: the rich cornfields of Anglesey, for instance, rapidly gave way to pasture in the second half of the nineteenth century, as supplies of cheap imported bread-wheat destroyed the home-based market.

Until the days of the earliest Neolithic communities, about 5000 years ago, the greater part of Wales had a fairly unbroken tree cover which fed and protected the underlying surface, an important factor in upland areas of thinner and less naturally fertile soils. As woodland cover was reduced during the Neolithic period, first by direct tree-felling and then by the inhibiting effect of grazing on woodland regeneration, these upland soils became increasingly impoverished, acidified and seasonally waterlogged; peat deposits began to accumulate in hollows and in a thin surface blanket over the more gently sloping upland areas. On the higher land much of this peat persists to the present day, but natural tree cover has virtually vanished from upland Wales, as well as from the richer farming land and intermediate pastures at lower level.

In looking at modern land use, and its affect on the country's 'aerial' archaeology, the colouring in the map on page 4 gives a reasonable indication not just of altitude but also of basic vegetation and land use. The lowland zones (green), up to about 150 metres above sea level, have relatively fertile light or medium soils supporting a mixture of dairy farming and stock-rearing, with occasional fields given over to arable cultivation for barley, wheat and root crops. There are more extensive areas of arable cultivation (though rarely amounting to more than a quarter of the local land use) on the central Borderland, and in parts of south Wales and Anglesey.

Between about 150 and 300 metres (brown) sheep-rearing predominates on managed pasture occupying heavier and more impoverished soils. Above 300 metres (purple), where the land is devoted almost exclusively to sheep-rearing, the soils are thinner, more acidic, and subject to periodic or permanent waterlogging. The more accessible parts have been extensively drained and 'improved' in recent decades by grant-aided ploughing and re-seeding to rape and for permanent pasture, though much of the land is now reverting to something nearer the rough pasture which it so recently replaced. The higher levels are dominated by bracken, heather moorland and rough mountain pasture. The only land use of significance here, apart from sheep-rearing, is conifer plantation, mostly dating from before 1980. Finally (coloured pink) there are the high moors and bare mountain tops which lie above about 600 metres, a delight to residents, visitors and mountaineers alike.

Flights into the future

While the underlying form of the landscape has been created by geology, glaciation, erosion and man's more distant use of the land, it is current land use that has the greatest impact on the 'aerial visibility' of the country's archaeology. This applies particularly to the cropmark archaeology which reveals so much that in non-arable areas may be hidden from us. It would be attractive to think that perseverance could eventually spread the benefits of cropmark archaeology to the whole of the country, but this will never be so, save for the occasional parching of pasture in times of extreme drought. The blanket of glacial clay that covers large areas will inhibit cropmark formation, and moist Atlantic winds will usually protect the western seaboard from the dry conditions that favour cropmark recovery. Even so, recent years have brought significant, if patchy, gains from cropmark photography in parts of the south and south-west, as well as in Anglesey and the Llŷn peninsula in the north; all of these areas had previously yielded little of the archaeology that lies masked beneath their plough-flattened surfaces.

In other parts of Wales, especially the less eroded uplands, more will come from progressively closer and better informed exploration of the landscape in conditions of low sunlight or snow, revealing features that on lower ground have been swept away by centuries of cultivation.

In both lowland and upland, too, a deeper understanding of the landscape, and of its forts, castles, abbeys and settlements, will come from the closer integration of aerial archaeology with the everyday activities of archaeologists and landscape historians in other fields, the academics of our universities and museums, the public servants of Cadw and the Royal Commission, and the conservation and rescue archaeologists of the National Parks, Local Authorities and regional Archaeological Trusts. In ten years' time, the picture of past and present in the landscape of Wales, seen from the vantage point of a light aircraft, may be very different from that presented in the tour of the country which makes up the remainder of this book.

South East Wales

Almost two thirds of the 3.5 million people of Wales live in the South East, in a sixth of the country's land area. Here, too, lies the bulk of the country's industry, particularly steelmaking, while the Bristol Channel coast has a string of ports which once served the now vanishing coal industry. There are also vast expanses of commercial forestry on high land in the north of the region, above a coastal plain that has brought agricultural wealth enjoyed by few other parts of Wales.

In the far west, beyond Swansea, lies the unspoilt coastal scenery of the Gower peninsula. Moving east, the high ground at first rises almost directly from the sea, but the landscape then opens out into the gently rolling farmland of the Vale of Glamorgan, mainly given over to dairy pasture now but heavily ploughed in the past and still carrying more arable cultivation than most other parts of Wales.

Further east, the suburbs of the capital city, Cardiff, extend into the foothills of the Carboniferous rocks that fringe the north of the region, etched by the narrow valleys of the South Wales coalfield. East of Cardiff and Newport the countryside broadens again into largely pastoral lowland in the valleys of the River Usk and its tributaries, with the mudflats and reclaimed land of the Severn Levels on the south, the Wye Valley and Forest of Dean on the east, and the lowering bluffs of the Monmouthshire Black Mountains to the north and north-west.

Archaeologically, the region has a rich spread of monuments across time: distinctive hillforts of the pre-Roman Iron Age, well preserved and accessible Roman sites, a wealth of fine castles, abbeys and country houses, and the ubiquitous traces of the Industrial Revolution.

Compared with much of Wales, however, aerial exploration here is in its infancy. Cropmark photography has yet to make a major impact, partly because archaeologists have not been in the air at critical times, partly because unresponsive clays discourage cropmark formation over much of the region. There is promise of rich returns, however, from low-light photography in the open countryside, and an exciting challenge for the air photographer in capturing the changing face of the industrial and urban landscape. The photographs on the following pages are just a beginning.

Left. *Newport Castle against the background of the modern town centre*
Top right. *Swansea, with the docks and the rejuvenated Maritime Quarter*
Right. *Cardiff Civic Centre, with the castle and Roman fort at top right*

Before the Romans

Moel Ton-mawr hillfort, Margam

Winter sunshine lights up one of the region's distinctive Iron Age settlements with widely-spaced ramparts. Both inner and outer enclosures are defined by a bank, ditch and slight external bank, with a stream completing the outer circuit on the left-hand side. The site occupies almost level ground on the high plateau above Margam Country Park and looks out over the western end of the Vale of Glamorgan. Conifer plantations like those seen here have transformed large parts of the Glamorgan uplands in the post-war years.

Excavation, field survey and casual finds show that the fertile lowland and flanking uplands of South East Wales were attractive to early man, from the later Palaeolithic cave-dwellers of the Gower coast, around 16,000 BC and earlier, through the first stages of shifting agriculture around 4000 BC, and into the more settled crop-raising and stock-rearing communities of the Bronze Age, between about 2000 and 700 BC.

The numerous burial mounds, or round barrows, of the Bronze Age show that both the high ground and the lowland were exploited at this time, in conditions significantly warmer than today. With rare exceptions (page 51), round barrows do not register particularly well from the air, nor - as yet - has air survey added to the little we know about the daily life and settlement patterns in the Bronze Age. The early date of some upland field systems has yet to be proven, and the fertile lower ground has inevitably been swept clean by later ploughing.

The 'aerial visibility' of daily life, throughout the whole of Wales, changes radically with the arrival of enclosed or defended settlements (loosely termed 'hillforts') in the first millennium BC, towards the end of the Bronze Age and through the following Iron Age. It may be that Continental ideas (though not necessarily folk movements) influenced this change, though the main stimulus may have been a climatic deterioration from about 1000 BC, driving arable cultivation and perhaps even pastoralism from the higher ground and bringing land resources at lower level under increasingly competitive pressure.

The variety of size, shape, location and grouping amongst these Iron Age settlements defies any single explanation, each region having its own distinctive patterns, both in the form of individual sites and in their distribution across the landscape. This is no less so in the South East than elsewhere. Just as the region's 600 or so Bronze Age barrows cover perhaps fifteen centuries of time, so the 120 hillforts must between them span ten centuries or more, up to the Roman conquest in the first century AD. By that time, we are told by the Roman historian Tacitus, South East Wales and perhaps much of Herefordshire was occupied by what he saw as a single 'tribe', the Silures, who for three decades resisted Roman domination before their final capitulation around AD 77.

For the most part, the Iron Age settlements on the Welsh side of the Border are relatively small in size, mostly enclosing four hectares (ten acres) or less. The Herefordshire sites are generally larger and more massively defended. Many of the Welsh sites, by comparison, occupy tactically weak locations, often with only a single bank and ditch for defence. Others, especially those that lie along the Bristol Channel coast, have multiple ramparts which in their time would have constituted strong and imposing defences.

A particular feature of the region is the wide spacing of the defensive earthworks at some of these settlements, the central area perhaps being occupied by dwellings, the outer enclosures by cattle and other stock when the need arose. Two such sites are shown here, along with two others restored to the record through aerial survey, thereby adding to our understanding of South East Wales in the thousand years before the coming of the Romans.

Tredegar Camp, Newport
Sandwiched between the M4 motorway and municipal housing on the fringes of Newport, this fine Iron Age fort provides a haven of open space within the urban sprawl. The wide spacing of the ramparts is common in the region but the massive scale of the second rampart is remarkable, especially alongside the modern housing. The earthworks may represent a single scheme of defence, or may be the result of development over time, a smaller and more angular enclosure being placed within a larger one of earlier date. At the centre is the terraced green of a long-abandoned golf course.

Two aerial discoveries south of Bridgend
Right. *In Ewenny Park a passing shot at the end of a winter flight reveals the ploughed-down traces of an oval enclosure, probably a simple hillfort of the pre-Roman Iron Age. The photograph makes sense of early, but previously unintelligible, references to 'earthworks' hereabouts.*
Far right. *At Tair Cross Down, alongside a modern road, the ditch of a similar enclosure is picked out by one of the few cropmarks so far recorded in the Vale of Glamorgan.*

The shape of Roman rule

The conquest of Wales by the Romans was an uneven and protracted process, involving repeated incursions between AD 48 and the final submission of the warlike Silures of the South East in about AD 77. From this time the region remained under tight military control through a network of auxiliary forts, linked by metalled roads to the legionary fortress at Caerleon, near the modern town of Newport. This pattern remained little changed until the middle of the second century, when a scaling down of the military presence and increasing evidence of acculturation and prosperity in rural settlements show that Roman economic life and civil administration had become firmly established. They remained so until the later years of the fourth century.

This picture is drawn mainly from excavation evidence, though air survey and the examination of air photographs already in public collections have made significant contributions, for example in identifying all fifteen of the region's known temporary or 'marching' camps from the years of military campaigning (two such camps from Central Wales are shown on page 137). However, a Roman route-list of the early third century, the *Antonine Itinerary*, makes it plain that at least one auxiliary fort in the South East, *Bomium*, still awaits discovery, probably near Cowbridge or Bridgend.

It is clear, too, that much of the road network and rural settlement pattern is still missing. There is a major role here for air reconnaissance and air photo interpretation, especially on the lower farmland, where temporary camps from the campaign period and rural settlements from later years doubtless await discovery through earthwork and cropmark photography. The unresponsive boulder clay that blankets much of the region will not ease the task, but encouragement may be drawn from cropmarks like those shown on the facing page.

Coed y Caerau: a Roman fort near Caerleon?
Shapes are often the aerial archaeologist's only guide to dating and interpretation. Here, above the M4 motorway near Caerleon, the 'playing-card' shape in the foreground invites interpretation as a Roman fort. The ridge-top situation would be ideal for the campaigning years, before the legionary fortress was built at Caerleon on low ground to the west. Alternatively, the rectangle might be a native settlement of the pre-Roman Iron Age, of a kind known from excavations in the Vale of Glamorgan. The irregularity of the more distant earthworks suggests pre-Roman origins, though a much rarer post-Roman date was proposed by the late Professor J K S St Joseph after he photographed the sites in 1959. Only excavation could reveal the truth.

Roman town of Venta Silurum, Caerwent
At Caerwent, the tribal capital of the Silures, the near-rectangular shape probably derives from the grid of streets and public buildings set out in the Roman fashion before the first earth and timber defences were added late in the second century. The fourth-century stone wall and bastions are among the most impressive sights of Roman Britain. At top right are the buildings of a 1940s propellant factory and later ammunition dump, eventually closed in 1993.

Roman amphitheatre at Caerleon

This striking and atmospheric monument was restored after excavations by Sir Mortimer Wheeler in the 1920s. The amphitheatre was built and repaired between the late first and mid-third centuries.

Fortress of the Second Augustan Legion, Caerleon

At Caerleon, near Newport, about half of the legionary fortress lies beneath the modern town, though much has been excavated since serious investigation began early this century. The layout of the fortress, which in about AD 74 replaced an earlier base at Usk, is explained in the Legionary Museum in the centre of the town, which has a spectacular display of everyday and unusual objects left by the legion's 5500 men between the late first and late third centuries AD. Parts of the fortress baths, barracks and defences have been set out for public display. The amphitheatre lies outside the fortress at lower left, alongside a parade ground, civil settlement and docks on an earlier course of the River Usk.

Rural settlements of the Roman period

*In the broader countryside we may imagine a pattern of small farms, fields and perhaps minor towns, though not on present evidence the major estates or 'villas' that typify Roman rural settlement in southern England. Excavation in the Vale of Glamorgan has, however, uncovered several rectangular ditched settlements which originated in the pre-Roman Iron Age but in some cases at least acquired ranges of stone buildings and a reasonable degree of prosperity during the Roman period. On the left, the twin ditches of a rectangular enclosure at **Cae Summerhouse, near Ogmore**, are outlined by cropmarks in the local drought of summer 1992. On the right, at **Caer Dynnaf, near Cowbridge**, the huddle of small buildings and yards along irregular streets, within the abandoned defences of the pre-Roman hillfort, seems more like a village than an individual farm.*

29

Castles in the history of Wales

Chepstow Castle
On its limestone bluff above the River Wye, Chepstow Castle, the earliest of Wales's masonry castles, evolved in four phases of construction, outlined in the excellent Cadw Guide to the site. The massive rectangular hall-keep at the centre, with stone-walled baileys in front and to the rear, constituted 'Chepstow 1', finished by William fitz Osbern, earl of Hereford, within a decade of the Norman landing in 1066. Over a century later William Marshal, earl of Pembroke, created 'Chepstow 2' by adding round-faced towers and a simple gateway to what is now the wall between the middle and lower courts. Before 1245 William's sons made 'Chepstow 3' by extending the keep, building a tower and gateway in the upper court, and strengthening the castle with the distant Barbican Court and the foreground Lower Bailey, its twin-towered gatehouse now facing visitors across the castle green. Finally, in 'Chepstow 4' (1270-1300), Roger Bigod III brought himself to financial ruin in adding a third floor to the keep, along with domestic quarters and the massive splay-based Marten's Tower in the lower bailey.

From the air the masonry castles of the Middle Ages are among the most dramatic sights of Wales. Their earth and timber predecessors can be equally striking, as is shown by the pictures on pages 145-7. But in this section it is the more intricate and impressive stone castles that hold our attention.

Within months of the battle of Hastings, William the Conqueror had the greater part of England under his control. To contain the unruly princes of Wales he created a series of Marcher ('border') lordships, with major castles at Chester, Shrewsbury and Hereford. From these initial strongholds, of earth and timber in the first instance, the Marcher lords pushed quickly into parts of north-east, central and south-east Wales. By 1094 their control stretched, on the lower land at least, along most of the southern seaboard, as far as Pembroke and Cardigan in the west.

Despite a fierce Welsh response in the next four years, and fluctuations thereafter, this pattern held for the better part of two centuries, the Welsh princes and the hardy pastoralists of the high country being strong enough to resist domination but too riven by feuding to achieve lasting unity, even in the major princedoms of Gwynedd in the north-west, Powys in the east and Deheubarth in the south-west.

Not until well into the thirteenth century did Llywelyn ab Iorwerth of Gwynedd ('Llywelyn the Great') and his grandson Llywelyn ap Gruffydd ('the Last'), bring the greater part of native Wales to some kind of unity and independence. But the arrival of a strong king on the English throne put an end to this. Edward I unleashed fierce reprisals in 1276-77 and again in 1282-83, killing the younger Llywelyn, dividing the north and west into 'shire' counties under the English crown, and with his barons constructing a network of massive stone castles throughout the whole of Wales.

By the early fourteenth century the great days of castle building were over. Twice more, however, they featured in the affairs of Wales, first in the revolt of Owain Glyndŵr

around 1400, when even Newport Castle was taken and burned, and again in the Civil Wars of 1642-49, when several castles in South East Wales did duty on the side of Royalist or Parliamentarian, Raglan holding out longer than any other castle in the land.

Thereafter, for most castles, came decline and decay, though some found new or continuing life as homes of the nobility. Later, the Romantic Movement in the late eighteenth and early nineteenth centuries inspired an enduring interest in their crumbling ruins, culminating in increasingly serious study and conservation during the present century.

Caldicot Castle

Caldicot Castle sits on a low ridge in once marshy land near the Severn Estuary. Its massive circular keep, on the right, has soil heaped against its base in the appearance of a motte. This kind of keep came into use around 1200, the shape making it less vulnerable to missile attack and undermining than the rectangular keeps of earlier years. The rest of the fabric is late, with some modern additions. The aerial view, however, gives a fair impression of what such castles must have looked like in their heyday, with the great hall and other buildings ranged against the flanking wall of the central court.

Caerphilly Castle

At Caerphilly a vast expanse of water, and complex outworks at front and rear, give the castle enormous strength despite its low-lying situation. The 'concentric' inner and middle wards on the central island, and most of the stone-faced dam in the foreground, were built in less than four years from 1268 by Gilbert de Clare, the local Marcher lord, during disputes over control of the Glamorgan uplands with Llywelyn ap Gruffydd, Prince of Wales. The castle was meticulously restored by the marquesses of Bute between 1869 and 1939.

31

Cardiff Castle, Roman fort and National Stadium

Cardiff Castle, in the centre of the country's capital city, has medieval fabric which re-uses the bold rectangle of a fourth-century Roman fort. The position alongside a crossing of the River Taff commended itself equally to William the Conqueror, who in 1081 may have set up a castle and a mint here following treaty discussions further west. To him, or to Robert Fitzhamon a dozen years later, belongs the basic layout of the castle, with its massive water-fringed motte at lower left. Timber buildings on the motte were replaced in the twelfth century by a stone 'shell-keep', linked by a covered stairway and bridge to an inner ward in the nearer third of the Roman fort. A massively banked and ditched outer ward took up the rest of the Roman fort, providing cover for troops and supplies, and for buildings serving the castle's many administrative functions. The towered buildings at lower right are domestic apartments of the fifteenth and sixteenth centuries, heavily remodelled in the eighteenth century, and again between 1868 and 1927 to create an exaggerated but successful neo-Gothic castle. In this last renovation, by the marquesses of Bute, the long-buried walls and gates of the Roman fort were uncovered and rebuilt, albeit a storey too high, to form the towered and battlemented re-creation that greets the visitor today.

The smaller picture shows the castle with the National Stadium at Cardiff Arms Park. Rapidly changing urban scenes of this kind are equally worthy of recording from the air.

Ogmore Castle

Like many other castles, the spectacularly sited Ogmore Castle, close to the Bristol Channel coast near Bridgend, occupies a strategic position as a frontier post and guardian of an important river crossing. First built in earth and timber, it is one of the most attractive and easily visited castles of South East Wales.

The castle's form betrays its beginnings as a ringwork and bailey, built in the first few years of the twelfth century on the western edge of the Norman appropriation at that time. A little later a rectangular stone keep, prominent in the larger view, was built beside the entrance into the ringwork from its seaward bailey, which never acquired stone defences. Early in the thirteenth century the palisaded bank of the ringwork was replaced by a simple curtain wall in stone, with a long rectangular hall on the northern side above the waters of the River Ewenny.

Long before then the castle had lost its importance as a frontier post, and it lacks any features typical of the late thirteenth century, such as a twin-towered gate or projecting towers to provide flanking fire along the curtain wall. A square, cellared building and a smaller set of 'offices' survive as foundations in the inner ward. A better-preserved stone hall of the fourteenth century in the bailey may have served as a court-house.

Village, house and garden

The photographs on this and the facing page were taken by one of the pioneers of air photography, the late Professor J K S St Joseph of Cambridge University. These pictures, and many others throughout the book, pay tribute to Professor St Joseph, and to his successor, David Wilson, for their exploration and recording of the Welsh landscape since the end of World War II.

The 1974 photograph on the left shows a village, now radically changed, in the visually striking setting of the Severn Levels. On the right the focus is on houses and their gardens, with two photographs from a series taken in 1951 of the great houses of South East Wales. At this time their patterns of estate management and self-sufficient gardening, revived to some extent during the war, were already coming under pressure in the peacetime years. More recent photographs of these once-fine estates often show deep inroads of decay and redevelopment, obscuring the original pattern and giving these early photographs a special historical importance.

St Brides, Wentlooge, and the Severn Levels
Although a church, and presumably a village, existed here by the early eleventh century, most of the present pattern is fairly recent. But there are hints, from earthworks in the large field on the right, of more extensive settlement in earlier times, perhaps with a small motte at the near end of the village and a rectangular moat or manor house at the far end. The whole of the field has been built over since the photograph was taken in 1974.

A special merit of the picture is its spectacular rendering of the surrounding landscape, the drained and reclaimed peat deposits and former mudflats which line the Bristol Channel coast between Newport and Cardiff. Drainage and land management were probably well advanced here by the Roman period. Indeed, drainage channels containing Roman material extend well beyond the present foreshore into the intertidal zone, where storm damage recently uncovered rectangular timber buildings which have been dated by tree-ring analysis to the fifth century BC.

Old Beaupre Castle, near Cowbridge

Old Beaupre, seat of the Basset family from around 1300, saw Elizabethan alterations before sale and decay a century later. Terraces beyond the house, in the past seen as a deserted medieval settlement or abandoned orchards, may actually be the formal gardens of the house, set out above fishponds and water gardens along the River Thaw.

Hensol Castle, near Cowbridge

This country mansion north-east of Cowbridge dates from about 1700, with alterations and additions in the nineteenth century. A special feature of the picture, taken in 1951, is its rendering of the walled kitchen garden and the lean-to greenhouses, derelict now but still in full production then, beyond the rear courtyards of servants' quarters and stables.

St Fagans Castle, near Cardiff

This gabled Elizabethan mansion of the Herbert and Lewis families, later owned by the earls of Plymouth, is now a much visited part of the Welsh Folk Museum. The emphasis in this 1951 view lies on the formal gardens recreated in the 1850s, probably over an earlier pattern, with new stone-walled terraces overlooking even earlier fishponds half-hidden by the trees in the foreground. The lawn to the left of the house shows the cropmarks of an earlier layout, now restored by the Museum, each quadrant divided into four beds around a circular centre. Former garden layouts of this kind can often be recorded from the air in times of drought.

Monastic life

Early in the twelfth century the traditions of the early Celtic church began to give way to a new pattern, with substantial communities committed to the religious life, though not always to priestly work in the world at large. Just as the Anglo-Norman lords, and later the Welsh princes, created castles to secure their secular control, so they endowed churches and monasteries to enlist a higher power. The monastic life, principally within the *Rule* of the Benedictine order, was already well established in England, though its early asceticism had become veiled by wealth, comfort and involvement in worldly affairs. Wales, in its turn, was colonised by monastic houses, not only of the Benedictines but also of the reformist Cistercians and the travelling priests of the Augustinian order.

The monastery buildings suffered gravely after the Dissolution in the reign of Henry VIII. Many vanished through systematic stone robbing, though others achieved fame as romantic ruins in the changed sensibilities of the late eighteenth and nineteenth centuries. In the present century, excavation, air photography and close study of the remains have created a new interest in monastic life and in the history of individual religious houses, from foundation to dissolution 450 years ago.

Cistercian Abbey at Tintern
Ever since the days of the Romantic Movement in the late eighteenth century artists, scholars and tourists have been attracted to the ruins of Tintern Abbey, set in the wooded and winding valley of the River Wye. The Cistercians, known as 'white monks' from the colour of their habit, tried to re-establish the simple religious life lost in part by the increasing wealth and worldly involvement of the older Benedictine order. Founded in 1131 as a colony or 'daughter house' of the Abbey of L'Aumône, near Chartres, Tintern began life as a community of perhaps twenty choir monks and up to fifty lay brothers (see facing page). In the later thirteenth century the unassuming church built by the monks a hundred years before was first surrounded, and then replaced, by the massive and ornate abbey church which dominates the view today. On the left lie the foundations of the abbey's conventual buildings - dormitories for the monks and visitors, refectory, kitchen, chapter house, abbot's quarters and infirmary for aged and sick brethren. Somewhat unusually, these are situated on the north side rather than to the south of the abbey church, around two open courts or cloister garths. The ruins of the church and its conventual buildings serve as reminders of the life of a monastic community from its beginnings in the twelfth century to its dissolution four hundred years later.

Augustinian Priory at Llanthony
In the Black Mountains of north-east Monmouthshire sunlight strikes through the nave arcade of Llanthony Priory (1108-1538) and picks out the grassed foundations of the priory barn in the foreground field. Unlike the Cistercians, the so-called 'black canons' of the Augustinian order were all full members of the priesthood, preaching regularly in local churches and around the priory's many possessions in Ireland.

Monasteries met their worldly needs in a variety of ways. Long before the Dissolution the majority were dependent for their daily necessities and considerable wealth on gifts and endowments from wealthy benefactors; these included land or church holdings in which the peasant farmers or parishioners ceded a portion, or 'tithe', of their annual produce. The monks were ruthless in claiming their rights, and legal disputes, violence and intimidation were common, even between rival religious houses.

The houses of the Cistercian order, however, at least in their early years, were more self-reliant. The brethren were divided into 'choir monks', fully committed to the contemplative life, and up to three times as many 'lay brothers', who were mainly concerned with construction work, crafts and general service at the monastery or on the community's outlying farms, or 'granges', like that at Monknash, illustrated below.

Cistercian Abbey at Neath

Neath Abbey was founded in 1130, one year before Tintern, which it closely resembles in plan, though with the conventual buildings on the more usual south side of the church. Parts of the monks' quarters were reused as a mansion of the Herbert family in the sixteenth and seventeenth centuries. Other parts became a centre for copper-smelting and ironworking in the early decades of the Industrial Revolution.

Monastic grange at Monknash *(right)*

Monknash grange, near the Bristol Channel coast, thirty kilometres from the mother house at Neath, retains the clearly defined boundary of its central farm which was the focus of a large estate of meadow and arable land. The earthworks, thrown into relief by low evening sun, include trackways, building plots, yards and possibly gardens, orchards and fishponds. Toward the centre stands a circular dovecote, and on the near side can be seen the walls of the great barn (above) in which were stored the produce of the farm and its outlying fields.

Birth and death of an industry

The Industrial Revolution and its insatiable appetite for fuel brought wealth and tragedy to the valleys of South East Wales: wealth mainly to the mine-owners, tragedy too often to the miners in the tight-knit communities that grew up around each pit.

By the later Middle Ages the region already had a long history of ironmaking, using readily accessible ores and timber at the heads of the valleys that divide the Carboniferous limestone of the southern uplands. From the late sixteenth century, however, ironmaking moved beyond supplying purely local needs to exploit markets elsewhere in Britain and beyond. Two centuries later came the full impact of industrialization. Many copperworks were established around Swansea and Neath, and a chain of ironworks grew up at the heads of the valleys, now using coke - and hence coal - as their fuel in place of charcoal. The advent of steam-power for the blast furnaces accelerated the process, and by 1850 there were ironworks across the whole of South Wales, from Pontypool in the east to Pembrokeshire in the west. During the next fifty years, with the introduction of large-scale production of steel by the Bessemer process, the focus moved down the valleys, and in 1891 reached the very heart of Cardiff, with the construction of the East Moors works. Tinplate production, meanwhile, became strongly established further west, especially at Llanelli and in the Neath and Swansea Valleys.

These developments had a dramatic effect on the extraction of coal. Until about 1830 the process was led by the needs of the local ironworks. After this, there was a rapid expansion to meet rising domestic demand and to satisfy an increasingly lucrative export market. From small surface workings and short shafts or tunnels the pits became progressively deeper and more complex in the search for the richer seams of coking coal and anthracite. In the latter half of the nineteenth century the mining valleys were opened up along their full lengths, with a peak production in 1912-13 of fifty-seven million tons, most of it exported through the docks at Cardiff and Barry.

After nationalization in 1947 there followed a period of consolidation and modernization, many old mines being closed or combined with neighbours, and new pits being sunk. Later came accelerating decline, as workable seams became deeper and more difficult to reach, and imported coal cheaper and more readily available. By 1975 only about forty collieries remained, and early in 1994 Tower Colliery, the last of the British Coal deep mines in South East Wales, ceased production. Apart from a handful of opencast and privately owned workings, and a single deep mine in North East Wales, an industry that once employed 250,000 men - a quarter of the country's workforce - is dead.

Mardy: a colliery vanishes
Mardy No 4, at Maerdy, the last operational colliery in the Rhondda Fach, closed a year after the upper photograph was taken in 1990. By January 1992 (left) it had been virtually erased from the map. On the foreground crag in both views stands Castell Nos, a Welsh castle of the twelfth or thirteenth century.

Merthyr Vale and Aberfan, near Merthyr Tydfil
*By the time this photograph was taken, in March
1990, Merthyr Vale colliery was already under
demolition, though the winding-gear and much of
the washing plant still stand at centre-frame. Most of
the railway sidings which linked the colliery to
Cardiff by way of the Taff Vale Railway (left, below
houses) have already gone, as has the overhead
ropeway which carried waste across the River Taff
and the neighbouring village of Aberfan to the
hillside beyond. Here, in November 1971, over a
hundred children and their teachers died when the
primary school was engulfed by slurry from the tips
above. Some of the houses of Aberfan, terraced
along the slope, are seen across the River Taff at top
right. By contrast, the terraces of Merthyr Vale (left)
are stepped up and down the steep valley sides. The
colliery has now entirely gone, leaving nothing but a
black expanse like that seen at the former site of
Mardy colliery (opposite).*

Taff Merthyr colliery, near Merthyr Tydfil
*Taff Merthyr colliery, an all-electric mine, opened in
1923 and lifted its last coal in November 1992. The
mine retained much of its original buildings and
equipment and was the subject of detailed recording
by the Royal Commission before and after its
closure. Demolition began in March 1994.*

Former colliery site, Abercynon (above)

At Abercynon, alongside the improved trunk road from Cardiff to Merthyr Tydfil, the colliery buildings have already vanished, to be replaced by the usual expanse of levelled colliery waste. Still prominent down the centre of the photograph is the line of the former Taff Vale Railway, along which coal was carried from this and many other collieries to the docks at Cardiff and Newport, now much reduced from the days of their greatest activity. The serried ranks of small terraced houses in the villages of Abercynon and (farther away) Carnetown, along with schools and chapels, are typical of the mining valleys, contrasting strongly with the conscious planning and relatively spacious design of the Oakdale 'model village', shown on the facing page.

Oakdale colliery and 'model village' (right)

The imposing horseshoe of the miners' village at Oakdale, near the eastern end of the South Wales coalfield, was a product of the Garden City movement of the early twentieth century, one of several planned housing schemes in Wales that arose indirectly from the Housing Act of 1909. Built between then and 1924 to house miners employed when the Oakdale Colliery was sunk, the village was laid out on level ground above the mine, here glimpsed in the middle distance in 1990, shortly after its closure. The relatively spacious layout of the houses, streets and public spaces at Oakdale contrasts starkly with the cramped and tightly packed terraces, without adequate drainage or water supply, built elsewhere by mine owners in the middle and later parts of the nineteenth century.

Patterns of industry

From the air, the patterns of industry are often breathtaking in their simplicity or convolution. Examples could be multiplied a hundred times from the landscape of South East Wales.

Waste-tips at Clydach Terrace, Bryn-mawr (right)
Waste-tips from ironstone extraction on the northern edge of the South Wales coalfield. The curving gully near the top marks extraction along a seam of coal.

Aluminium works at Waunarlwydd, Swansea (left)
The Alcoa works is one of the last survivors in Swansea's long tradition of metal processing.

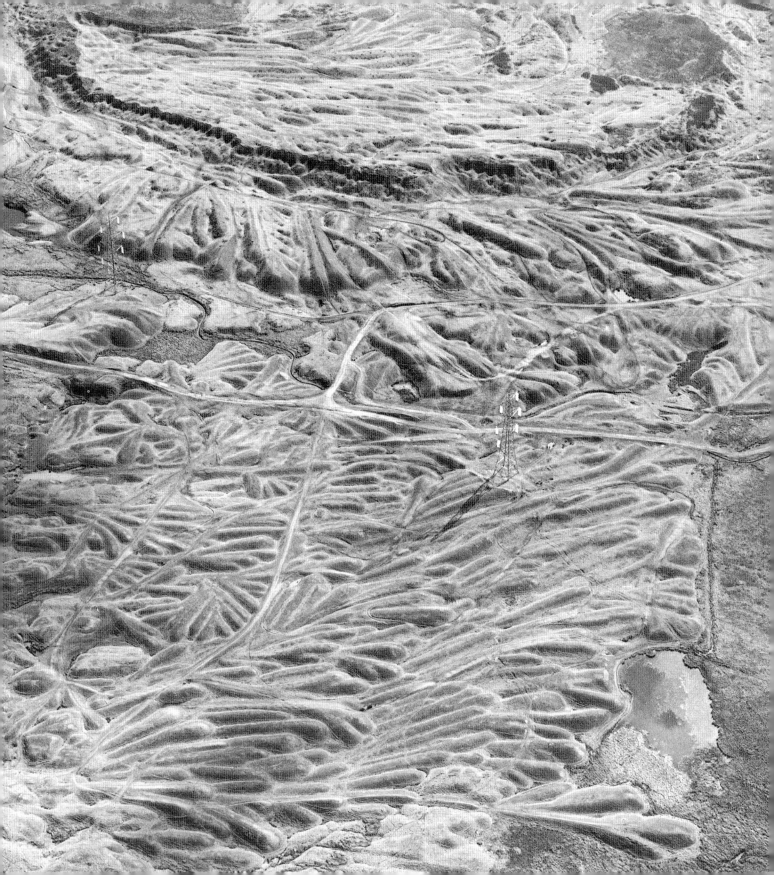

Swansea: a city remakes itself

Swansea and the Gower peninsula present an unrivalled microcosm of Wales's past. Nowhere else in the country are there such concentrated riches, whether viewed from the ground or from the air. Many of the finest historical sites, too, are readily accessible, and set in surroundings of great natural beauty.

Swansea itself, *Abertawe* in Welsh, is a city of outstanding historical interest. To its west the Gower peninsula is blessed with sheer limestone cliffs and secluded bays on the south, long strands and spectacular headlands in the west, and wild sand-dunes and saltwater marshes along the north. Away from the coastline gently rolling pasture gives way with startling suddenness to tracts of bracken-covered or heather-clad 'upland', though little of this higher land rises more than 200 metres above sea level. Within this most variable of landscapes are set easily visited sites of all periods save the Roman, from occupied caves of the Upper Stone Age to castles and industrial monuments of the present millennium.

Swansea's name (*Sveins-ey* = 'Sweynes's island' or 'inlet') suggests that the settlement may have begun as a Norse trading post some time around the tenth century AD. Swansea only enters written history, however, with the creation of the Anglo-Norman lordship of Gower, soon after 1100. A strong earth and timber castle, just beyond its stone successor in the picture opposite, was in existence on the west bank of the River Tawe by 1116. Around it grew a thriving town and port, protected from the early years of the fourteenth century by a now vanished town wall. Swansea formed the administrative centre, or *caput*, of the Gower lordship. It was also the lordship's main centre of craftwork, trade and seafaring, exploiting wharfage along the eastern side of the town and enjoying tidal anchorage at the wide mouth of the River Tawe.

By the late sixteenth century Swansea was exporting not only dairy goods, cattle, sheep and hides but also quantities of coal from the rich seams that come close to the surface along both sides of the Tawe Valley. It was, indeed, this combination of seaborne access, plentiful water and ready supplies of coal for fuel that gave Swansea its prominence from the early eighteenth century - and later its pre-eminence - in the field of copper smelting and distribution. Ore from Cornwall, and later from Anglesey and elsewhere, was smelted at Swansea and shipped to Bristol and other centres for manufacture. Soon the sides of

North Hill Tor and the Whitford Point lighthouse
The saltwater marsh beyond the relict cliffline of the north Gower coast, seen over the defences of the medieval castle ringwork of North Hill Tor. The view stretches across the sand dunes of Whitford Burrows to the disused cast-iron lighthouse of 1865, itself now a protected ancient monument.

Swansea Castle and the modern city centre (left)
The picture shows the former site of medieval Swansea, with the fourteenth-century castle just right of centre, next to the telephone exchange tower. The earlier castle of the twelfth century lay just beyond its successor, with the medieval town spreading to top right and lower left in this view.

the Tawe Valley to the north of the town became a forest of copper
smelting works, supplying nine-tenths of Great Britain's refined copper
by about 1800. By this time copper working had been joined by the
smelting of lead and zinc, and in the middle years of the century there
was added the rolling and tinning of iron and steel to make tinplate, much
of it for export to North America.

For much of the nineteenth century Swansea maintained its world
importance as a metal-processing centre. Inevitably, however, there
came decline. As the century wore on the copper-smelting industry came
under increasing pressure as good quality ore became more difficult to obtain. Tinplate, too, suffered when tariffs were placed on
imports into the United States in 1890. After a partial recovery before
and during the First World War, the next three decades saw the Swansea
Valley lose its industrial base in successive cycles of boom and
bust. Soon after the end of World War II the bulk of the once-teeming

tinplate mills and all but one of the copper-smelting works had become
empty shells, their crumbling stacks set in a wasteland of polluted slag
heaps and decaying industrial housing.

The city, too, suffered heavily in the war, its centre devastated by a
three-day blitz in February 1941. Post-war rebuilding swept away even
more of the medieval street pattern. In the 1960s reclamation began on
the poisoned industrial wastelands, unfortunately before air photography
or ground survey could properly record the legacy of the city's former
industrial supremacy. Today the reclaimed areas have sprouted sports
facilities, parks and light industry, while the formerly deserted South
Dock, in the heart of the city, has found new life as an attractive and
successful waterside redevelopment.

Swansea may never regain its central place on the world stage, but it is
once more a thriving and developing city, set in countryside of abiding
beauty.

Pembroke and Milford Haven
The viewpoint emphasizes the defensively strong position of Pembroke Castle and the fine anchorage provided by the broadening waters of Milford Haven.

South West Wales

Apart from a narrow lowland strip in the south, where the railway snakes along the coast from Swansea and Llanelli to Carmarthen, the south-western peninsula and the Cardigan Bay coast are separated from the rest of Wales by the rugged hills of the Cambrian Mountains, from Plynlimon in the north to the Black Mountain in the south (page 21). To the west, the landscape is gentler, though a tongue of higher land projects along the northern side of the peninsula to create Mynydd Preseli and the rocky headland of St David's.

Carmarthenshire, in the south-east of the region, includes a band of industrial development around the steel town of Llanelli, behind which the broken country of the Coal Measures is scarred by underground and surface coal-workings and backed by the higher ground of the Black Mountain, itself pitted by centuries of quarrying, mainly for lime-burning.

Further west, in Pembrokeshire, the higher ground of Mynydd Preseli looks out to the south over a gently undulating lowland plateau, which falls steeply to the sea around the deeply indented coast; its cliffs and coves have been designated since the 1950s as the Pembrokeshire Coast National Park.

Cardiganshire, north of Mynydd Preseli and the curving valley of the River Teifi, has a rather different scenery, rising from the coastal sweep of Cardigan Bay in a series of 'steps' or narrow plateaux, dissected by east-west valleys and backed by the upland pasture and open moorland of the Cambrian Mountains.

Away from the industrial areas in the south-east, the region's economy relies largely on dairy farming, with sheep and forestry on the higher ground, and tourism especially along the coast. Apart from potato growing in Pembrokeshire there is little arable cultivation. This might suggest meagre returns for the aerial archaeologist from cropmark photography. In recent years, however, the pattern has changed as locally-based flying has brought a closer focus onto the scattered arable fields and - most fruitfully - the broader areas of parched grassland in times of prolonged summer drought.

The industrial areas and the central uplands deserve more attention from the air, but there is already an embarrassment of riches. Prehistory offers distinctive Iron Age settlements, while Skomer provides an ancient landscape to match any in Britain. Roman Carmarthen adds a tribal capital and tantalizing new discoveries from the air. The Middle Ages have St David's cathedral and a fine series of castles and historic towns. More recent times give rediscovered gardens and the lead-mining landscapes of north Cardiganshire. As these pictures show, air photography has already made a distinctive contribution in South West Wales, and this will surely grow over the years as the broader landscape enjoys the benefits of intensive study from the air.

The Cardiganshire landscape north of Aberystwyth
From Penrhyn-coch Camp to the Cambrian Mountains.

The townscape of industrial Llanelli
Medieval settlement around St Elli's church (top left) has vanished beneath the nineteenth-century and modern town.

Pembrokeshire in prehistory

The south-western peninsula of Wales - Pembrokeshire and the western parts of Carmarthenshire - has a rich prehistoric archaeology, much of it well recorded, and an increasing amount of it first discovered, from the air. To the east and north the traces of pre-Roman occupation are more thinly spread, as has been the pattern of aerial exploration so far.

As well as having many fine burial chambers, once concealed within the round or elongated mounds of Neolithic communal tombs of about 4000-3000 BC, the area is unique in Wales in possessing an excavated settlement site of the Neolithic period, on the rock outcrop of Clegyr Boia, near St David's (left).

A recent 'aerial' addition to the region's early archaeology is a pit-circle (below) close to Withybush Aerodrome, at Haverfordwest, from which many of the recent flights over the area have been made. Only excavation could show whether the pits of this unusual discovery belong to a Late Neolithic timber circle, like that recently investigated at Welshpool (page 127), or to a long-demolished circle of stones from the succeeding Early Bronze Age (2000-1200 BC).

In the South West, as elsewhere in Wales, farmsteads or other settlements belonging to the Bronze Age are few and far between, though the round barrows which contain the burials of the period are a frequent feature of the upland scenery; a few, too, are now coming to light as cropmarks in more lowland situations.

Round barrows of the Bronze Age often occur in groups, perhaps used over many generations by the same tribe or family group. One of the most spectacular groups in Wales lies at the heart of the fine Iron Age hillfort of Foel Drygarn, seen opposite in the dying light of a summer's evening.

Neolithic settlement at Clegyr Boia (above)
Amid the rows of plastic covers that protect early Pembrokeshire potatoes, this rocky crag west of St David's has a double claim to fame, as one of the few British sites with Early Neolithic houses, and as the fabled stronghold of an Irish pirate, Boia, whose death is recounted in the 'Life of St David', written in the eleventh century. Neolithic structures, both rectangular and circular, were found during excavations at the far end of the crag, along with characteristic pottery and other objects typical of the Neolithic period. Uncertainty, however, surrounds the date of the stone-faced rampart which turned that part of the rock into a small but sturdy stronghold. Its deeply recessed entrance is faintly reminiscent of Iron Age hillforts on the Borderland. Alternatively, the rampart might belong to the Neolithic period, though it was clearly later than **some** *of the Neolithic pottery found during the excavations. Then again, we must not forget Boia, on his rocky stronghold in the sixth century AD.*

Pit-circle at Withybush, Haverfordwest (left)
Low evening sun casts shadows where the crop has grown taller along the curving line of a former stream bed or sunken trackway and beyond it are thirty or so pits of a circle about sixteen metres in diameter, discussed in the main text above.

Cairns at Foel Drygarn, Mynydd Preseli (right)
Near the eastern end of Mynydd Preseli the disturbed stone mounds of three massive Bronze Age round barrows stand within the rampart of this fine Iron Age hillfort, which is alternatively known as Moel Trigarn (the name means 'the hill of the three cairns'). There is an outer enclosure around part of the circuit (lower right) and a further 'annexe' beyond this at lower left. The hillfort and parts of the outer enclosure are pock-marked by levelled 'hut-platforms'. Excavations in the early 1900s produced Roman as well as Iron Age finds.

Hilltop fort at Carn Ingli, Newport (left)

Near the western end of the Preseli Hills stands Mynydd Carn Ingli, an open ridge of heather, whinberries and bracken, crowned by the jagged rock of Carn Ingli itself. Here, legend has it, St Brynach, of nearby Nevern, conversed with the angels, and thereby gave the site its name, 'Carn Ingli', the Mount of the Angels.

Legends apart, Carn Ingli has its own mystery in the strange fortifications that encompass the rocky outcrop and spread down its scree-strewn flanks. Some time in the past the loose stone of the crag was built into a formidable wall round the long triangle of the summit, itself divided by cross-walls into four linked enclosures, the widest and lowest at the left in this view. On the far side of the crag extra walls form two steeply sloping outer enclosures. In these, and on the near-side slopes, the tumbled scree has been shaped into a network of small soil-filled terraces, presumably for crops or tethered animals.

Within the fort are further terraces, pathways, enclosures, hut-platforms and individual buildings, both round and rectangular. The impression is of a small but well-protected hill-settlement, long-lasting to judge by the complexity of the enclosing walls, which may first have ringed just the topmost crag, before spreading along and over the ridge as the pressure of population grew. Up to nine narrow gaps in the wall give easy access to the terraces and gentler slopes below, though all could have been quickly blocked in times of danger.

Carn Ingli's combination of features makes it unique in Wales. It has been assigned variously to the Neolithic, the Iron Age, and the post-Roman periods. Quite possibly it belongs to all three, in a pattern of repeated reuse and adaptation.

Coastal fort at Flimston Bay, near Pembroke

Pembrokeshire has a wide variety of Iron Age hillforts, including many along the cliffs and promontories of its lengthy coastline, where they can be readily seen from the long-distance path of the Pembrokeshire Coast National Park. One that is particularly spectacular from the air, but has limited access from the ground, lies above Flimston Bay, within the Castlemartin RAC Range south-west of Pembroke. Here a double line of bank and ditch, tripled to the left of the centrally-placed entrance, is supplemented by another line further out to cut off a promontory that has been carved by wind and sea into an extraordinary convoluted shape. The interior is marked by recessed 'hut platforms', which would have held roundhouses and buildings of other shapes, probably of timber, during the lifetime of the fort.

Open settlement on Mynydd Carn Ingli, Newport

As at Carn Ingli itself, uncertainties surround a complex of embanked fields, enclosures, trackways and scattered round-huts (or ring-barrows) on the slopes north and north-east of the hillfort. Some parts must be prehistoric, others are perhaps medieval or even later, like the stone-walled sheepfold inside an earlier enclosure at upper right. A small roundhouse or ring-barrow lies at lower right.

A distinctive feature of the south-western peninsula is the rash of small embanked enclosures that lie between the scattered hilltop forts of the pre-Roman Iron Age. Generally circular or oval in shape and thirty to sixty metres across internally, they mostly occur in hillslope or lowland situations.

The hillforts and enclosures, however, could cover a considerable span of time, a point addressed in recent excavations by the Dyfed Archaeological Trust. A dense group of sites near Llawhaden, in east Pembrokeshire, were shown to range in date from the Late Bronze Age, around 1000 BC, to the Roman period, over 1000 years later, each being used for a few hundred years, some more, some less, and some with periods of abandonment and reoccupation. By and large, the hillforts were early, while the smaller enclosures belonged to the immediate pre-Roman centuries, or in one case even to the Roman period itself.

In recent years the already dense distribution of such settlements has been further increased by a growing number of aerial discoveries, especially between Carmarthen and Haverfordwest and on the coastal plateau near Cardigan. Many of the newly discovered sites are ditched enclosures, resembling the surviving earthworks in form and in their preference for hillslope locations. Some also display outer lines of defences and entranceways that have all but vanished from the surviving earthworks. One such is pictured on the facing page, to show the kind of discovery that can be made when drought entices cropmarks from a region previously thought unresponsive to this kind of aerial photography.

Gelli Camp, Llawhaden
A superficially simple 'small enclosure' alongside the Carmarthen to Fishguard railway, with a narrow entrance at upper right. In fact, cropmark photographs show a ditch-lined passageway running from the entrance towards the railway. Faint earthworks in this view would be too indistinct for reliable interpretation without the cropmark evidence. An eroded bank to the left suggests another enclosure in the same field.

Summerton Camp, Mynydd Preseli
Summerton Camp's inner enclosure measures about forty metres across (like Gelli Camp, above). Here, however, an outer enclosure provides extra protected space. The banks are strongest alongside the entrance gaps on the uphill, left-hand side. The less distinct breaks to the right are probably recent creations to improve agricultural access to the site. The inner enclosure would probably have held a small number of timber roundhouses, along with storage buildings and other structures belonging to a farming community of perhaps a single extended family.

Cropmark enclosure at Rhiwau, near Llawhaden

In hilly country on the border between Pembrokeshire and Carmarthenshire, this fine cropmark enclosure typifies recent aerial discoveries in showing a relatively small and strongly ditched inner enclosure, surrounded by a wider but more narrowly ditched outer one. In some cases the narrowness of the outer cropmark suggests the foundation for a palisade rather than an open ditch.

Here, the entrance gaps are linked by the shadow of a sunken track that continues towards the bottom of the picture. Other sites have entranceways that are lined on either side by the cropmarks of ditches or palisades. In some parts of Britain 'antennae' of this kind have been seen as a device to channel stock into the inner enclosure. However, the Dyfed Archeological Trust has excavated similar features on nearby sites, where the inner enclosure was undoubtedly reserved for people rather than animals. In South West Wales, it seems, the aim was to provide an imposing and well-protected entrance for human visitors rather than the control of stock.

In some cases the cropmarks of concentric outer ditches or palisades have been photographed around small enclosures that survive as upstanding earthworks. It seems possible that many apparently simple enclosures, like Gelli Camp on the facing page, may originally have had outer enclosures that acted as the 'home fields' or protected stockyards of the Iron Age farmsteads that they represent. The region's cropmark enclosures take a variety of shapes, including simple rectangles, often with an entrance on one of the narrower sides. In one case excavation showed that a rectangular cropmark pre-dated the enclosing bank of an oval enclosure, raising the possibility that some of these rectilinear marks may represent the long-sought Bronze Age occupation sites of the region.

Skomer: an island landscape

The island of Skomer, twenty minutes by boat off the western tip of Pembrokeshire, delights visitors with its scenery, plant life, seals and birds, especially in May when the bluebells and other flowers are at their best and the puffins are tending their young. The island also preserves one of the most complete and accessible ancient farming landscapes in Britain, readily viewed from the footpaths that criss-cross the island's National Nature Reserve.

Climbing from the landing point onto the central plateau, visitors look across to the near-island known as The Neck, its right-hand tip marked by the rampart of a small promontory fort, probably pre-Roman in date. At the north-eastern end of the island most of the ancient fields, which may date from as early as the Neolithic period or as late as the pre-Roman Iron Age, are defined by sloping 'lynchets', created by the accumulation of plough-soil against the boundary with a lower field. Elsewhere, the divisions are made of earth and stone, often robbed now of their smaller boulders for use in the field walls of Old Farm, which worked the central parts of the island from the eighteenth century until 1948.

Dispersed among the ancient fields are the foundations of small circular huts, sometimes single, sometimes situated in small groups. There are also stock enclosures, cairnfields (some of them perhaps cemeteries, others created by the clearance of stone from the surrounding area) and even dams along one of the island's streams. The fields probably once supported a mixture of arable cultivation and the rearing of sheep, cattle and possibly pigs. At the height of this early occupation, perhaps lasting no more than 100 years, or perhaps much longer, the island may have been home to a self-sufficient community of up to about 200 men, women and children.

Ancient fields on Skomer Island
At the north-eastern end of the island, a pattern of ancient fields is seen in the left foreground, with the larger stone-walled fields of Old Farm to the right. Beyond the narrow isthmus the most prominent feature is the rampart which cuts off the right-hand promontory to form the small fort known as South Castle.

A field wall on Skomer Island
At the western end of the island most of the ancient field divisions consist of large stones and boulders, of the kind shown here. Smaller stones gathered from the fields alongside would once have made them effective boundaries.

Ancient fields and huts on Skomer Island

The most compact group of ancient fields lies on the northern side of the island. The oval enclosure at lower left was probably the original focus of settlement here; two circular huts stand against its left-hand side, one clearly marked, the other less distinct. Two other groups of huts lie in the corners of fields near the centre of the picture. Many of the fields show traces of narrow ridge and furrow cultivation, possibly created by a primitive plough. A stone ploughshare of the kind that might have been used was found in one of the island's several ponds.

Old Farm, Skomer Island

Old Farm and the northern side of the island are seen here under bluebells in the early part of May. Old Farm now houses a small exhibition illustrating the island's plants, wildlife and archaeology.

The edge of Roman rule

The apparent lack of forts and authenticated Roman roads west of Carmarthen has perpetuated the idea that the local people, known to the Romans as the *Demetae*, acquiesced in the Roman advance into South West Wales in the mid-70s AD. At all events, a fort was established at the lowest bridging point on the navigable waters of the Tywi, on the site of modern Carmarthen. There grew up alongside the fort a civilian settlement which developed after reduction of the military presence into a thriving tribal capital, *Moridunum*. The Roman settlement, clearly visible in the fabric of the modern town, has been explored in recent years by the Dyfed Archaeological Trust, whose former field officer, Terrence James, took the fine view of the town on the left and first recognized the Roman road pictured on the right.

What happened in the immediate post-Roman centuries is not entirely clear, though a Welsh settlement certainly existed around the eastern (far) end of the Roman town when the first Norman castle was established to its west in the early 1100s. The castle quickly acquired its own defended town, with quays and wharves on the riverfront nearby. The importance of Roman *Moridunum* was matched by the medieval borough of Carmarthen, which became one of the most populous and prosperous towns of Wales.

Despite occasional finds of Roman pottery and coins, and antiquarian speculation about roads to the west, the pattern of Roman influence west of Carmarthen is only now beginning to emerge. The presence of Roman material on recently excavated native sites in Pembrokeshire causes no surprise; rural settlement must, after all, have continued through the Roman period.

But a major development has been the recognition on vertical air photographs of a Roman road running west from Carmarthen, perhaps to a landing point on the river near Haverfordwest or on the west coast near St David's. This discovery, augmented by oblique photography in 1991 and 1992 (right), has prompted new thoughts about conquest, settlement and travel in South West Wales during the Roman period and in the centuries that followed.

Carmarthen and the Roman town of **Moridunum Demetarum** (left)
Modern streets still outline the sub-rectangular shape of the Roman town (R) which grew up alongside the auxiliary fort (F) established on the west bank of the Tywi in the mid-70s AD. Beyond the town lies the Roman amphitheatre (A) and the medieval Priory of St John (P), sited within a native Welsh settlement. The medieval castle (C) and its planted English town (M) occupied an area to the south-west of the Roman town, with quays on the river below, out of view.

Roman road west of Carmarthen (right)
From a slightly curving line in the foreground, parched grass above the gravel make-up of the road can be traced intermittently into the far distance. Both in the foreground, and in the next field, where the road itself is barely visible, there appear the darker marks of flanking pits from which the gravel make-up was quarried. Some of these survive as distinct hollows to the present day.

From hermit's cell to bishop's palace

The Celtic saints of the fifth to seventh centuries hold a special place in the traditions of the Christian church, though firm knowledge of them remains obscure. The eleventh-century *Life of St David*, upon which so much hangs, may have been aimed more at encouraging pilgrims, and the gifts that they brought with them, than at the factual recording of earlier events.

Unfortunately, the archaeological evidence for any aspect of the period, beyond church dedications and memorial stones, is disappointingly weak. Few domestic sites have yet been identified, while the hermits' cells, chapels and monasteries which may be inferred from the historical record have almost all vanished or been obscured by later events at the sites they once occupied.

There is only legend to connect St Govan's Chapel (left) with the hermit saint of that name, though his cell is said to have stood here before the present well-chapel was built in the thirteenth century. The strange earthworks on Gateholm Island (below) may represent the cells of a monastic community, but excavation has yet to show that this is so.

By contrast, there is no doubting the early origins of St David's, where the bishop's palace and other splendid buildings make this one of the finest cathedral precincts in the whole of Britain. Here the medieval walls of the cathedral close may well follow the much older boundary of a monastic settlement, dating from as early as the sixth or seventh century AD.

St Govan's Chapel
A thirteenth-century chapel on the traditional site of a hermit's cell, in the sea cliffs south of Pembroke.

Dark Age settlement on Gateholm Island (left)
The little strings of rectangular huts or 'cells' on Gateholm Island, off the south-western tip of Pembrokeshire, are unique in Wales. Once interpreted as a Romano-British village, they may alternatively have belonged to a monastic or secular settlement of the fifth to seventh centuries, as suggested by a brooch with Irish affinities found in one of the huts in the 1930s.

St David's Cathedral and Bishop's Palace (right)
Hereabouts, near his reputed birthplace, St David is said to have founded his first monastery in the sixth century, before travelling widely in south Wales, Ireland and beyond. The church burned down in 645 and later suffered at the hands of the Danes, but it became such a revered place of pilgrimage that in 1120 the Pope declared two visits to St David's equal to one pilgrimage to Rome. The present cathedral dates largely from the late twelfth century. The walls of the cathedral close, begun a century or so later, still retain one of their gates, the twin-towered Porth y Tŵr of about 1300, seen at lower right against the Lady Chapel of the cathedral. The sumptuous lifestyle enjoyed by the medieval bishops can be judged by the decorative grandeur of their now roofless Palace, at upper left.

Castles and historic towns

When the Normans swept into the South West in the last decade of the eleventh century, along the Bristol Channel coast and through the mountains of central Wales, their first move was to establish castles at strategic points such as river crossings and coastal landfalls. Over the following years, as the struggle for control ebbed and flowed, castles proliferated throughout the region, and the Welsh too began to adopt this form of defensive building. As a result the South West developed a density of castles approaching that of the eastern Borderland, whose mottes and ringworks are illustrated on pages 145-7.

Like most Conquest-period works, these early castles were of earth and timber rather than stone, though no less effective for that in the conditions of the day. But the emphasis over the next few pages is on the stone successors beneath which these early earthen castles now lie hidden, and on the defended towns that grew up - or were 'planted' - around what were significant administrative and legal centres as well as military strongholds.

In the first instance the towns, and the commercial activities that they nurtured, were usually protected by substantial defences of earth and timber, though in the thirteenth and fourteenth centuries many boroughs were given strong stone walls. A few of these imposing walls survive remarkably intact to the present day - at Tenby, for instance (page 75), or at Caernarfon in North West Wales (page 91).

Elsewhere, the medieval walls and gates have vanished, though their positions can often be traced in the street patterns of the present day, or can be reconstructed from the fine series of town maps made by John Speed around the year 1610. By Speed's day, however, many of the towns had followed their castles into semi-desertion and disrepair, sadly reduced from the bustle and commercial prosperity of their medieval heyday, and far removed from their early military origins.

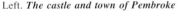

Left. *The castle and town of Pembroke*
Pembroke Castle sits at the tip of a promontory between two streams, off an eastern arm of Milford Haven (page 48). An earth and timber castle was founded here in 1093 during the first Norman onslaught on the South West. The position proved well chosen, and the castle never changed hands until its final surrender to Cromwell in 1648. The castle we see today was built by William Marshall, earl of Pembroke, between 1189 and 1219. A distinctive feature is the lofty round keep, based on French models and the earliest of its type in Britain. To a large extent the impregnability of the castle accounts for the success of the town, which spread quickly along the promontory, its single street lined by narrow ownership plots, or 'burgages'. Many of these survive to the present day, as do parts of the town wall. Prosperous throughout the Middle Ages, Pembroke had a population of around 1000 in the early fourteenth century.

Carreg Cennen Castle, near Llandeilo
On its spectacular limestone crag above the Tywi Valley, Carreg Cennen was initially a Welsh castle, held in the early thirteenth century by the princes of Deheubarth. It later changed hands several times and the surviving fabric dates from the end of the century, following the campaigns of Edward I. The isolated position was ideal for a military fortress but not for a town, and Carreg Cennen remained no more than a castle throughout its life. Within an outer ward now reduced to its foundations (front and right in this view), the castle sits four-square on the summit of the crag. Its shadowed inner ward and domestic apartments were approached through a barbican entrance, to the right, along a stepped ramp broken by two drawbridges, before a turn across a third bridge to the castle's inner gate. The rectangular foundation in the foreground was first noticed from the air, though its purpose remains unknown.

The castle and town of Kidwelly

The coastal castles of Kidwelly, Llansteffan and Laugharne, all of them readily supplied from the sea, were vital to the Normans' struggle for control of the Carmarthen area in the early twelfth century.

The castle founded here around 1110 by Roger, bishop of Salisbury, was a D-shaped ringwork set above a steep fall to the Gwendraeth Fach. Some of the stonework in the castle's outer wall probably belongs to this period, or at least pre-dates the late thirteenth-century reconstruction which gave the castle its present form. Then, a corner-towered inner ward was built within the original ringwork, the walls of which were augmented to form the outer ward. The castle thus became one of the finest 'concentric' designs of this period, its tall innermost walls and towers commanding the much lower but still formidable wall of the outer ward. The twin-towered outer gate in the foreground of the smaller picture dates from the fourteenth century.

The town of Kidwelly first developed in the large southern bailey of the Norman ringwork, beyond the castle in the larger view. A second bailey, on the near side of the castle, remained unused, its bank visible between the river and the road at lower right. The town expanded rapidly, and settlements quickly grew up beyond the south gate, on the right, and on the opposite side of the river beside the Benedictine Priory of 1114. The spire of the priory church is just visible on the left-hand edge of the picture. Of the town's thirteenth-century walls only small sections now remain.

From the air, the pattern of Kidwelly's development is clearly seen in the fragmented nature of the present-day settlement, while the castle remains one of the finest and most intelligible in Wales.

Carew Castle, near Pembroke

Carew Castle reputedly belonged first to Rhys ap Tewdwr, prince of the Welsh kingdom of Deheubarth, who passed it to Gerald of Windsor, the constable of Pembroke Castle, on the latter's marriage to Rhys's daughter, Nest, in 1110. In fact, Gerald himself may have built the castle, as an eastward outpost of Pembroke. Whatever the castle's origin, it would initially have been of earth and timber, the first stonework (of the recessed tower on the near wall) being erected around 1200, and the bulk of the castle dating from a century or so later.

Carew Castle has a special interest for the alterations and additions made in the Tudor period by Rhys ap Thomas, who held a famous tournament here in the early years of the sixteenth century. Later in the century Sir John Perrot constructed a vast three-storey range along the right-hand side of the castle, its large mullioned windows facing onto the river below. These alterations turned the castle into a sumptuous country residence, complete with walled courts and gardens in the foreground and terraces on the lower ground beside the river.

Excavations in the 1980s showed that the castle's outer ward, just beyond the foreground ditch, lay over an earlier promontory fort, defined by five deep ditches cutting across the spur. These are clearly visible as cropmarks in the smaller photograph, taken from the opposite direction in 1949. Air photographs of this kind offer archaeologists help in planning their excavation strategy, even before the first turf is turned.

The castle and town of Cardigan (left)

Cardigan Castle lies hidden and inaccessible in a clump of trees at the end of the bridge which it has guarded since the castle was first constructed in earth and timber during the twelfth century. It was rebuilt in stone in the middle of the next century. Little of the accompanying town wall now remains visible, though its line can be traced from John Speed's map of 1610, and from the alignment of present-day property boundaries. The town wall enclosed an oval area extending from the castle to a curving row of houses at centre left. Beyond this the road to the north sweeps right in the Victorian and later suburbs. Of the Benedictine Priory which once stood on the riverside east of the town, only the church now survives, at top right.

The castle and town of Haverfordwest (right)

At Haverfordwest the masonry successor to the earth and timber castle of about 1110 is readily visited, alongside the town's Victorian gaol and County Record Office. The earliest 'planted' town, a Flemish settlement, lay beyond and to the left of the castle; it included the town's first market place, and the church of St Martin (top left). In the thirteenth century the town expanded into the foreground and was given stone gateways, becoming one of the largest and most prosperous medieval boroughs in Wales. Redevelopment has transformed the riverfront, where the Benedictine Friary stood from the early thirteenth century on a site to the right of the narrow medieval Bridge Street, seen here running away from the small square in the foreground.

67

Lost gardens rediscovered

Air photography can offer striking illustrations of country houses, set in their landscaped parks and gardens. It can also 'rediscover' older gardens, all but lost to the changing fashions of the day. The view of Gregynog on page 14, for instance, shows former paths and flowerbeds picked out by drought in the manicured lawns of the present day.

Sometimes, by contrast, it is the house itself that has vanished, though usually leaving some documentary evidence to pinpoint its former location or to explain physical traces that have been rediscovered on the ground or from the air. This is true of the gardens illustrated here, which were targeted initially from documentary research. Later study showed that both belonged to the same wealthy and fashionable Pembrokeshire family, the Owens of Orielton, around 1700 when they were probably laid out.

The study of Welsh historic gardens, and of the more 'genteel' aspects of the countryside from about 1400 to the present day, has only just begun. To judge from these early results of aerial survey we can expect exciting discoveries in the coming years.

Historic gardens at Coedcanlas and Landshipping

'COEDCANLAS ... [medieval to] 17th-century house ... field before it, called 'The Old Garden' ... looks important.
LANDSHIPPING ... major 17th century house ... in ruin by c1800+ ... all gone now save part of red-brick walled garden ... water folly here in 1696 ... aerial view has potential.'

So concluded Thomas Lloyd of Cresselly in October 1991 from his research into Pembrokeshire houses. But it was 1993 before low winter sunlight allowed photography that corroborated Mr Lloyd's research.

At Landshipping (left) the walled garden stands close to the road at the top, with the house once nearby. In front are the raised beds and terraces of the lost garden, a rectangular pond at the centre flanked by a chevron of raised beds and on the left by the positions of individual trees in a vanished orchard or arboretum.

At Coedcanlas (above) a large rectangular enclosure, overlying ridge and furrow cultivation, looks across a possible water-garden to smaller plots set out along a raised terrace. An engraving of about 1710, showing a similar layout at Ashurst House, at Highgate in London, suggests that the large rectangle was probably a walled pleasure garden, with the smaller plots on the right given over to vegetables, though still decoratively arranged.

On the evidence from Coedcanlas and Landshipping, Pembrokeshire in the early eighteenth century could offer gardens as fine as any in Britain.

Coastal defences at Milford Haven

The deep inlet of Milford Haven (page 48) provides one of the finest deep-water anchorages in the British Isles. As such, it has assumed a new role in the last forty years as the destination of bulk tankers bringing crude oil to onshore tanks and refineries, like that at Rhoscrowther (below). From the air, however, there are powerful reminders of the Haven's longstanding strategic significance, and of past efforts to secure it from attack (right, and over page).

Although distant from the heartland of England, the south-west coast of Wales has throughout history enticed invaders and travellers from abroad. In 1405 Owain Glyndŵr landed French mercenaries at Milford Haven, and in 1484 Henry Tudor used the same route on his way to Bosworth and to the English crown as Henry VII.

The need to defend the Haven from sea-borne attack was first recognized by Thomas Cromwell; later, in 1580, 'blockhouses' were begun at the outer entrance to the inlet. Two centuries after this the threat of invasion from France provoked renewed efforts to protect the deep-water anchorage, along with the Naval Dockyard newly established on the northern shore at Milford (whence it was later moved to Pembroke Dock). As the power of steamships and on-board guns increased in the

Nineteenth-century fort at Popton Point, Milford Haven
Gun batteries on the right were backed by heavily defended barracks on the left. In and beyond the fort are the emplacements of oil-storage tanks, now removed.

Texaco Oil Refinery and Milford Haven
The town of Milford, on the far side of the Haven, was the site of the Naval Dockyard until 1814.

early nineteenth century, successive schemes of defence were conceived, the latest involving self-contained forts which had batteries to command the sea-borne approaches and heavily defended barracks to guard against encirclement from the rear.

The result was the Haven's network of almost indestructible coastal forts, built at vast expense between about 1850 and 1870. In the event, the forts were never put to the test, losing their military relevance as tactics turned towards mobile rather than static gunnery over the following thirty years. By the turn of the century almost all were derelict, though many were re-manned and modified for sea and air defence during the First and Second World Wars. From the air, their stark geometry provides a reminder of the military ideas of another age.

Milford Haven and Pembroke Dock: the geometry of defence

Top left. *The star-shaped Defensible Barracks at Pembroke Dock, built in 1844-45 to protect the town and Naval Dockyard which stood on lower ground to the north. Largely derelict since the early 1900s, the Barracks now provide an imposing clubhouse for the South Pembrokeshire Golf Club.*

Bottom left. *The circular bulk of Stack Rock Fort, built in the 1860s on a small island in the centre of Milford Haven, has at its centre the darker oval of a smaller tower belonging to a somewhat earlier fortification. The fort was originally planned to have two floors of gun emplacements, but was redesigned to convert one level into barracks for the fort's permanent garrison of troops.*

Right. *The strict rectangularity of the naval town of Pembroke Dock, established in the first half of the nineteenth century after the Naval Dockyard was moved from its original site at Milford, further to the west on the northern side of the inlet.*

Aberystwyth and the mining of lead

The university town of Aberystwyth, facing the broad sweep of Cardigan Bay, has prehistoric and Roman remains close by and a Dark Age monastic site at nearby Llanbadarn. The Normans built an earthwork castle on a hilltop to the south, and another early castle probably lies somewhere beneath the modern town. Later, Aberystwyth was used by Edward I for one of the strategic castles of his campaigns of 1276-83.

The town's more recent history was based on sea trade from its tidal harbour and, after the seventeenth century, on the rich mineral resources of the nearby hills. The Cardiganshire lead and silver mines, and the smelting and metalworking that went with them, brought prosperity to the town, especially in the nineteenth century. As the century wore on, however, decline set in, the mines being forced to exploit ever deeper deposits in the face of cheap imports from abroad.

The history of the mines is one of remarkable enterprise, dashed hopes, wealth or ruin for the owners and investors, and squalor and early death for the miners and their families. In some ways the rise and fall of the mines is well documented, but study of their physical remains consistently offers new insights. Increasingly, too, air photography is helping archaeologists to record and understand these industrial remains of the relatively recent past.

The castle and town of Aberystwyth
In the foreground the diamond-shaped castle of Edward I, built in 1277-89, has been released by recent excavations from the tumbled stone of its own collapse. To its left, facing the sea, is the curving facade of the old University building, in origin a villa designed by John Nash, which was later extended as a prestigious hotel. The new university campus lies on the hillside at the top of the picture. The layout of the streets beyond the castle and the church of St Michael reflects the gridded pattern of the 'planted' town established alongside the castle, though the medieval town walls have long since vanished. The harbour, so important to the post-medieval lead industry of West Wales, lies outside the picture to the right, beyond close-set terraced housing of the nineteenth century.

Pendinas hillfort and Aberystwyth
This fine Iron Age hillfort, dominating the harbour and town beyond, probably began as a single-banked enclosure on the lower and more distant hill. Later, multiple defences took in the foreground hilltop, and the intervening saddle was also enclosed. The column on the summit was erected in 1852 to commemorate Wellington's victory at Waterloo.

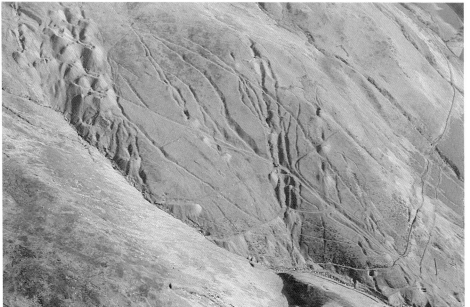

Cwmystwyth lead mine

Deep in the hills to the east of Aberystwyth, the Cwmystwyth mine was for much of the nineteenth century one of the most productive lead and silver mines in Britain, though its opencast and underground workings have lain deserted since its final closure in the 1930s. This view illustrates the importance of the mine's many leats, running along the lower part of the hillside to bring water from higher up the valley to the mine's pumping, lifting and crushing machinery.

Copa Hill, Cwmystwyth

Sledge-inclines and deeply scoured 'hushes' on Copa Hill, at the eastern end of the Cwmystwyth mine. Here the target mineral was copper. The hushes were worked by releasing water from storage dams above the mine to wash away overburden and loosened rock from the ore, which was then worked in opencast trenches. The more 'upright' hushes at the centre of the picture appear to include workings that date from the Bronze Age, in the second millennium BC, though there was clearly exploitation at later periods also.

A contrast in resorts

Tenby and Saundersfoot, on the south coast of Pembrokeshire, are neighbouring resorts with very different histories.

Tenby is first mentioned in a Welsh poem of the ninth century. Two centuries or more later it acquired a Norman timber castle, later rebuilt in stone. In the Middle Ages it became a thriving town and port, trading by sea along the Bristol Channel and beyond. Its fortunes waned after the Elizabethan period, but the nineteenth century brought revival as a resort for high society. More recently rail and the motor car have extended its popularity. Through all these changes Tenby's walls and medieval street pattern have survived largely intact, above the picturesque harbour and beaches that ensure its continuing prosperity.

Saundersfoot, by contrast, was very much a nineteenth-century creation, for the export of anthracite from the now-vanished Pembrokeshire coalfield. Its harbour, crowded in summer with yachts and pleasure craft, was once linked directly to the pits by the Saundersfoot Railway, itself long dead though still strikingly visible from the air as it winds its way through the surrounding countryside.

Saundersfoot harbour and railway (above, left)

Anthracite mining began around Saundersfoot in the sixteenth century or earlier, but it was the 1830s before the Saundersfoot Railway and Harbour Company created a direct link from the pits to a loading point more convenient than the local beaches or the relatively distant harbour at Tenby. At first the railway was a horse-drawn operation, though it was re-laid for steam in 1874. One branch struck inland by way of a 'balanced incline', on which a linking cable allowed descending wagons full of coal to pull empty wagons back to the top of the incline. Another line ran down the main street of the village towards Wiseman's Bridge and Kilgetty. Tracks ran onto both sides of the harbour (right) and coal was loaded down chutes directly from the railway wagons.

In the picture on the left, looking south-east towards Begelly and Saundersfoot, the railway snakes its way through the fields from pits at Thomas Chapel. The railway enjoyed mixed fortunes, as did the pits. By the 1930s much of the line had been abandoned, and closure soon followed after the last mines were shut in 1939.

Tenby and St Catherine's Island (right)

The North Beach and harbour lie on the left, with the castle on the headland beyond. On St Catherine's Island, beyond the South Beach, stands the 1870s fort which formed part of the coastal defences of Milford Haven (pages 69-71). The tree-lined town wall, raised in 1457 from thirteenth-century beginnings, runs across the picture from a corner tower at lower left; a return wall and the vanished Carmarthen Gate once closed the gap above the North Beach on the left. Projecting from the wall at upper right is the semi-circular barbican of the West Gate, now called The Five Arches from the extra openings cut through it in the nineteenth century. At the centre, amid the street pattern of the medieval town, stands the imposing church of St Mary, reflecting the town's prosperity in the later Middle Ages. Most of the Elizabethan and earlier houses have given way to later buildings, including fine Regency terraces along the clifftop at the far end of the town. The buildings at lower right are relatively recent, development barely having spread beyond the medieval walls until the 1850s.

Llyn Stwlan, near Blaenau Ffestiniog in Snowdonia, a natural lake dammed for power generation

North West Wales

For visitors and residents alike the abiding image of North West Wales must surely be the mountainous crags of Snowdonia and the high land facing Cardigan Bay, the constant backdrop to a rugged and stone-walled landscape in which the present-day economy relies mainly on sheep farming, forestry and tourism. Memorable in different ways are the lowland plain and occasional arable fields of the north-coast island of Anglesey, and the embanked fields and craggy northern spine of the Llŷn peninsula in the far west. Along much of the seaboard the steep falls from the interior create distinctive coastal scenery, not least in the broad estuaries that strike inland from the northern sweep of Cardigan Bay.

In a small aircraft few experiences are more startling than turning from the low land of southern Anglesey to confront the rugged mountains of Snowdonia across the narrow and distinctively bridged Menai Strait. More than any other part of Wales the North West abounds in such scenic contrasts, and the local archaeology is equally varied and distinctive.

Although the castles of the Middle Ages, both Welsh and English, figure strongly in this aerial view of the region, there is also a proper emphasis on the upland archaeology of earlier times. Here, the lack of widespread cultivation in recent years allows a more complex interplay of ancient and modern land use than survives in most of southern and eastern Wales.

To the pictures of castles and upland landscapes there is added the remarkable view of a ritual complex of the earliest farming communities near Bangor, discovered from the air just in time for rescue excavation in the face of modern industrial development. Also shown from the aerial perspective are easily-visited Roman sites, the dramatic relics of the once great slate industry, and the equally striking remains of mineral extraction on the island of Anglesey.

In many ways the North West is the most exciting region of Wales for the aerial archaeologist. Here, most of all, the combination of aerial and ground-based exploration can aspire to a rounded understanding of the changing landscape, from earliest times to the very different realities of the present day. If landscapes rather than individual sites predominate on the following pages, this truly reflects the region's special archaeological character. Sadly, it also emphasizes how much archaeology may have been lost through ploughing and upland pasture improvement in the less rugged parts of Wales.

Bridges on the Menai Strait (top), *and the Mawddach Estuary from Barmouth*

Early ritual on the North Wales coast

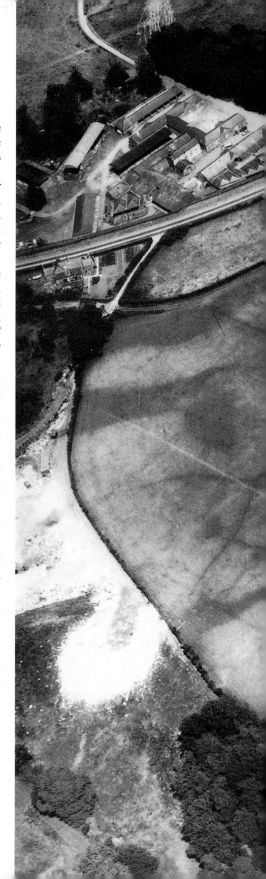

In the long dry summer of 1959 air photographers from Cambridge University made one of the most important discoveries of Welsh aerial exploration. On a gravel terrace on the outskirts of the north-coast town of Bangor, the Cambridge team photographed a dense concentration of cropmarks in a large cornfield, alongside the cricket ground at Llandegai.

As seen in this photograph, taken a year later, the main features were two large circular enclosures, one at upper left, its wide ditch marked by a narrow entrance gap on the near-left side, the other at lower right, its narrow ditch pierced by matching entrance gaps at top and bottom. A smaller and thinner circle was visible at lower left, whilst at upper right, 'emerging' from the oval of the cricket field, were the parallel ditches and rounded end of what could only be a *cursus* monument or ritual avenue of the Neolithic period.

Taken together, this was clearly a ritual complex of the Neolithic, and perhaps the Early Bronze Age, the large circles being ritual enclosures, or *henge* monuments, datable in other parts of Britain from around 3000 BC, the smaller circle probably the ditch of a round barrow or enclosed urnfield cemetery of a millennium or so later. Other lines traversing the field belonged to a road and field boundaries of relatively recent date, while the whole area was marked by an irregular network of 'frost-wedges', formed through freezing and unfreezing of the soil in periglacial conditions after the end of the last Ice Age.

Unknown to the Cambridge photographers, the area had already been designated for industrial development. But the discovery was so important that a few years later the field saw the largest rescue excavation undertaken in Wales to that date. The excavations, in 1966 and 1967, stripped the recent plough-soil from large parts of the field and confirmed the identification of the henge monuments and cursus. As usually happens on cropmark sites, however, the work also revealed other traces not visible from the air, including apparently domestic structures underlying the slighter (and later) of the two henges, and pre-dating both. Also uncovered by the excavations were two other funerary or ritual ring-ditches, and a small cemetery of Christian burials alongside a timber-built chapel; this may have been the earlier church said to lie 'within two bowshots' of the fourteenth-century church of St Tegai, which stands just beyond the limits of this picture.

The left-hand henge, an imposing monument which originally had an internal bank within a massive ditch nine metres wide and almost four metres deep, held further surprises in that it had been reused much later for a long-lived settlement which at one stage had at its centre a sophisticated timber-built roundhouse fifteen metres in diameter. Also present were four-posted structures, conventionally interpreted by archaeologists as store-houses for grain or other foodstuffs.

In the absence of datable pottery or metalwork this secular reuse of the henge monument can only be assigned to the later Bronze Age or the succeeding Iron Age, from around 1200 BC to the Roman conquest in the first century AD. There is a hint of a relatively late date, however, since the still substantial bank of the henge had been deliberately levelled over the remains of the settlement, perhaps by the Romans to obliterate what may still have been an important focus of native occupation (and possibly resistance). A native settlement of the Roman period, quite different in character, later grew up over the almost vanished traces of the henge.

Despite the uncertainties of a rapidly organized rescue excavation, staffed mainly by volunteers, this discovery and its follow-up remain one of the most dramatic achievements of aerial exploration and rescue archaeology in Wales.

Cropmark complex at Llandegai, Bangor
The photograph has been printed dark in order to emphasize the cropmarks.

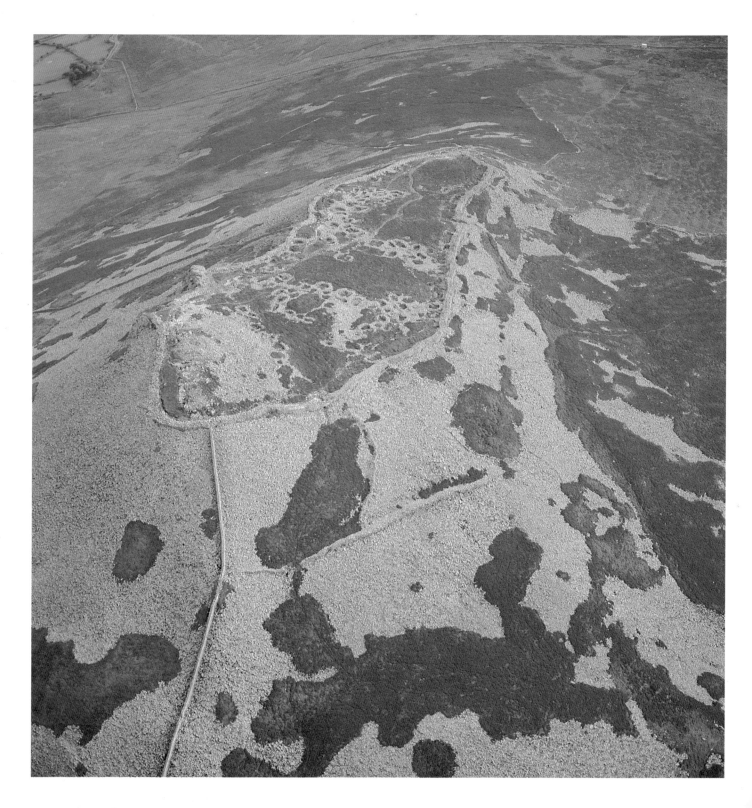

Hillforts, hutgroups, wandering walls

The traces of native settlement in the pre-Roman and Roman periods are more distinctive in the North West than in any other part of Wales. This owes much to the rugged and essentially non-arable nature of the landscape and to the widespread use of stone as the main building material, allowing walls and field boundaries to survive long after they would have vanished in more heavily cultivated parts of Wales, where timber and earth were the main materials of construction in antiquity. As a result, large swathes of ancient landscape can still be found in the upland areas, especially on the slopes overlooking the north and west coasts. In addition to a fine range of pre-Roman hillforts, the region has its own distinctive types of settlements - 'hutgroups', 'terraced fields' and 'wandering walls' - which perhaps reflect economic and social structures heavily conditioned by the rigours of the landscape.

The main difficulty in presenting a coherent picture of the region is the lack of reliable dating evidence, a common problem in the archaeology of Wales. Modern excavations have been few, though important work has been done in recent years. Moreover, the material culture before and even during the Roman period seems to have been relatively poor, the near-absence of native pottery and metalwork robbing archaeologists of their standard, if often unreliable, guides to dating. Only with the use of radiocarbon analysis to date charcoal have the pre-Roman origins of many long-lasting settlements become firmly established, though the majority (if producing any finds at all) still yield only Roman material.

It has also become clear that timber-built phases underlie at least some of the stone settlements, highlighting the archaeologist's difficulty (without excavation) in unravelling the history of settlement when only the latest, and perhaps most variable and complex, stages of development survive above ground. Here, as elsewhere in Wales, a coherent but no doubt locally varying picture will only emerge when carefully chosen excavations provide good dating and environmental evidence for key sites across the region. In the meantime, the aerial archaeologist has a growing role to play in illustrating the special features of the area, and in uncovering aspects of the developing landscape that have so far eluded fellow workers on the ground.

Tre'r Ceiri hillfort, on the Llŷn peninsula (left)
This dramatically-sited stone-walled fortress, with its tight clusters of stone-built huts, gives a good idea of what such hilltop settlements may have looked like during the pre-Roman Iron Age. Unusually, Tre'r Ceiri remained in occupation throughout much of the Roman period, many of the Iron Age roundhouses being reshaped to more rectangular outlines.

'Terraced fields' above the Nantlle Valley, near Caernarfon (right)
Overlain by modern walls and smoothed by recent pasture improvement, these 'terraced' fields originally grew up around unenclosed groups of stone-built huts, here (as elsewhere) barely detectable from the air. The terraced effect derives from the downslope drift of soil under plough-cultivation. The picture is taken from the archives of the Gwynedd Archaeological Trust.

Enclosed hutgroup, Ffridd Bod y Fuddau, near Trawsfynydd (above)
A typical small hutgroup of two or three stone-built huts, grouped together within an oval enclosure. A second enclosure, perhaps for stock, lies on open ground beyond the boundary wall. Narrow and irregular cultivation ridges in the foreground are a rare survival of early enclosure for plough cultivation, probably contemporary with the settlement.

'Wandering walls' settlement, Llyn Ogwen (left)

On the eastern fringes of Snowdonia above the trunk road from Betws-y-coed to Bethesda, a pre-Roman settlement, first identified from the air, occupies a south-facing slope over 350 metres above sea-level. The settlement's stone-walled roundhouses are barely visible, one of them obscured by a circular sheepfold, two others by a jumble of stone beyond a T-shaped sheep shelter. The 'wandering walls' may have aided periodic corralling of stock, or have arisen - even at this great height - from the clearance of stone from irregular cultivation plots in what must nevertheless have been a largely pastoral settlement.

Muriau'r Gwyddelod, Harlech (right)

Overlooking the west coast above Harlech, the area of ancient landscape known as Muriau'r Gwyddelod ('Irishmen's walls') shows how modern farming can unwittingly obliterate earlier patterns of land use. In places stone clearance and pasture improvement have removed all trace of the earlier fields, while elsewhere the walls and enclosures of 2000 years or more ago survive largely intact. In the foreground is a sub-circular enclosure with unusually thick walls, similar in appearance to the 'raths' of Ireland, and perhaps indeed an 'Irish' settlement. Beyond, in a patch of open ground, two 'enclosed hutgroups', of slightly differing form, and possibly of Roman date, are linked by a curving wall amid the general pattern of enclosures and 'terraced fields'.

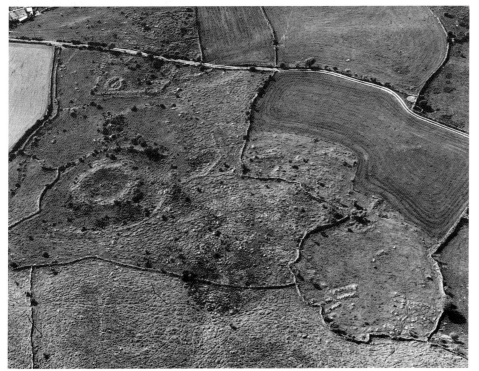

Hafoty Wern-las, near Caernarfon (left)

On gently sloping land near Caernarfon settlements of several periods draw on the same pattern of field enclosures. On the left is the distinctive outline of a pre-Roman 'concentric circles' homestead, which probably once had a timber-built roundhouse at its centre. Beyond, against the road, lies a polygonal 'enclosed hutgroup', a distinctive form of settlement which frequently yields Roman pottery and evidence of metalworking. Just across the road are several 'unenclosed' huts, while two oval hutgroups lie just beyond the picture at top right. At bottom right medieval or post-medieval settlement is suggested by two rectangular foundations, and a possible corn-drying kiln in a 'nick' in the field wall. The modern field walls on the left still respect lines first set out more than 2000 years ago.

84

Along Cardigan Bay between Harlech and Barmouth the land rises fairly steeply from the sea to an irregular plateau which supports one of the richest multi-period landscapes in Britain. From the Neolithic period onwards the plateau was used repeatedly by man, each new episode leaving its own imprint on a gradually more complex 'ancient landscape'. In recent years stone-clearance and pasture improvement have speeded the pace of change, so that parts of the pattern have now become obscured or lost altogether. Fortunately, the plateau's importance has been recognized by the protective 'scheduling' of selected areas, and aerial survey has begun to provide the overview that ground-based workers need if they are to unravel the complex relationship between natural and man-made features. Between Dyffryn Ardudwy and Barmouth the landscape is particularly complex, the overlay of prehistoric, native Roman and later occupation clearly visible beneath the more recent divisions which march up to the wall dividing the enclosed area from the open hillside beyond.

Landscape at Pen y Dinas, Dyffryn Ardudwy (left)
Here, the entrance passage of a small Iron Age hillfort, Pen y Dinas, is overlaid by the rectangular foundation of a medieval or post-medieval platform-house, one of its straggling enclosure walls cutting right the hillfort approach. At lower right, above the ravine of the Afon Egryn, stands the curving outer wall and recessed hut-platform of a pre-Roman homestead. At top right another enclosure and a pattern of ridge and furrow cultivation face onto the other side of the river gully. Much of the foreground is covered in grassed-over field clearance-cairns, along with a network of overlapping stone-edged enclosures which could only be fully understood through intensive survey and analysis on the ground.

Landscape on Is-Mynydd, near Barmouth (right)
On the area known as Is-Mynydd, north of Barmouth, three large oval or circular enclosures, each well over 100 metres across, lie close to one another in the middle distance. Two have inner enclosures with right-facing entrances; all were first recognized from vertical air photography. They are perhaps large versions of 'concentric circles' homesteads of the pre-Roman Iron Age. In the foreground there now appears a fourth large homestead, its central circle and outer enclosure too diffuse for recognition in ground-based surveys undertaken in recent years.

85

Roman forts and native homesteads

The first Roman incursion into North West Wales, around AD 60, saw the building of a short-lived fort somewhere on Anglesey. The task of pacification was to be delayed, however, until a disaster to a detachment of Roman troops some years later prompted a daring and successful campaign by Agricola, governor of Britain from AD 77 to 83. This campaign reasserted Roman control and, in the words of the historian Tacitus, 'cut to pieces almost the whole fighting force' of the local people, known to the Romans as the *Ordovices*.

To this assault, or to the period of consolidation that followed, we can trace the first days of the forts at Tomen-y-mur and Segontium (opposite and next page). At Tomen-y-mur the military presence lasted barely seventy years, but at Segontium it persisted in one form or another until the final decade of the fourth century AD.

Despite their initial worsting at the hands of Agricola, the native communities continued farming the surrounding countryside, though the rarity of early Roman finds suggests some resistance to - or perhaps exclusion from - the trappings of Roman civilization. The latter part of the Roman period, however, sees the full flowering of the settlement type known as the 'enclosed hutgroup', its variations perhaps reflecting differences of social status and life-style amongst the families who made their homes in these distinctive stone-walled homesteads of North West Wales.

Roman practice camps at Dolddinas, Trawsfynydd
Three of five miniature camps built by troops from the fort at Tomen-y-mur, each with rounded corners and entrance gaps at the centres of opposing sides.

Tomen-y-mur, Trawsfynydd: a Roman fort and its environs (right, opposite)
The Roman fort at Tomen-y-mur takes its name from the Norman motte or 'tomen' built over the fort's reduced defences 1000 years after its abandonment in the middle of the second century AD. The fort is remarkable in retaining the surrounding clutter of a Roman military establishment, notably a levelled 'parade ground' (P), and an overlooking mound or 'viewing platform' (V), in front of which is a narrow rectangular enclosure, probably medieval rather than Roman in date. Also visible in this view is a small amphitheatre (A), perhaps for weapons practice rather than games or animal displays. There are also traces of the fort's linking roads (R), one of them on a raised embankment (E) to carry it across a local stream. A rare survival is a sinuous leat (L), which once brought water from a nearby lake to a raised aqueduct that would have carried it across lower ground to the commandant's house and headquarters building within the fort. In the foreground are the ploughed-down remains of two small practice camps (C), while in the distance at top right are banks which almost certainly mark out enclosures associated with the fort, along with a large square mound assumed to hold the burial of one of the fort's senior officers or commandants.

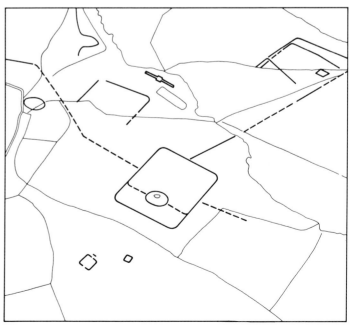

Caernarfon and the Roman fort of Segontium

About 1200 years before Edward I began his great stone castle at Caernarfon, the Romans chose a higher position nearby for what became the pivotal fort of their military hold on North West Wales. Its 'playing-card' shape now sits amongst modern housing and is bisected by the A4085 trunk road. Originally built in earth and timber for a garrison of 1000 infantry, the fort was occupied continuously, though sometimes by as few as 200 men, from its first construction around AD 77, through various rebuildings in stone to its final abandonment in the last decade of the fourth century.

Segontium, one of the most accessible and intelligible Roman forts in Britain, was first explored in the 1920s by R E M (later Sir Mortimer) Wheeler, then Keeper of Archaeology at the National Museum of Wales. The reconstructed foundations of the stone barrack blocks, headquarters building and comman-

dant's house can be seen in the right-hand side of the fort as viewed here, alongside the museum which holds many of the best finds from the site.

More recently, excavation in the left-hand end of the fort revealed an imposing courtyard building, with its own small bath-house in a private garden to the rear. This, the excavators argue, probably served through much of the second and the whole of the third century as the residence and offices of an imperial procurator, dealing with the rich mineral resources which made Anglesey and the North Wales coast so important to the Romans.

In the Roman period the far sides of the fort were flanked by a thriving civil settlement, while a cemetery lay in the foreground, alongside the parish church of Llanbeblig. Just right of the church in the 1950s there were found the remains of a Roman shrine to the Persian god Mithras.

Enclosed homestead at Dinllugwy, Anglesey

Dinllugwy, in north-east Anglesey, belongs to a class of stone-walled homesteads notable for their sharply polygonal outline and the relative richness of the mainly late Roman finds which they produce on excavation - relative, that is, to the near absence of domestic debris of any date on most north-western settlements. Dinllugwy and similar homesteads were probably the seats of powerful families or individuals in the local farming communities.

In this photograph by the Gwynedd Archaeological Trust the homestead is entered from the left through a rectangular building that forms a kind of gatehouse. The interior has both circular and rectangular buildings, the former probably for living, the latter for workshops, byres and the like. Here, as elsewhere, one of the rectangular structures was used for the working of iron.

Occupation at Dinllugwy, and at other enclosed hutgroups in North West Wales, may well have continued into the post-Roman centuries, though Dark Age finds are too rare to raise this beyond reasonable conjecture.

Homestead enclosure at Caer Lêb, Anglesey

Caer Lêb, in south-west Anglesey, is protected by twin banks and ditches, though the outer ditch is now largely refilled and its bank flattened on two sides. In the nineteenth century the site produced Roman pottery and metalwork, along with circular and rectangular buildings in stone. It may belong to a class of broadly rectangular enclosures peculiar to Anglesey and differing from enclosed hutgroups in using banks and ditches rather than stone walls for their enclosure.

A superficially similar site excavated recently by the Gwynedd Archaeological Trust began life in the pre-Roman Iron Age as a timber roundhouse within an irregular palisaded enclosure. In a later pre-Roman phase an imposing rectangular bank and ditch replaced the palisade, and a second timber roundhouse was added. During the Roman period one of the roundhouses was replaced in stone but the bank and ditch was allowed to fall into disrepair, leaving the site looking rather like Caer Lêb today.

The castles of North West Wales

There can be few sights more impressive from the air than the walled towns and castles which Edward I built across North Wales in the last two decades of the thirteenth century.

From the beginning of the century the fortunes of the north-western Principality of Gwynedd had revived under Llywelyn ab Iorwerth ('Llywelyn the Great', 1173-1240) and later under his grandson Llywelyn ap Gruffydd ('Llywelyn the Last'), who had succeeded as sole ruler by 1255. The unity now established in the lands ruled by the Welsh princes was eventually recognized by Henry III in the treaty of Montgomery of 1267, which secured for Llywelyn the title of 'Prince of Wales' and recognized the existence of the Principality of Wales.

But the accommodation was an uneasy one and the outcome was inevitable when Llywelyn persistently refused to fulfil his obligations to Edward I as his overlord after Edward succeeded to the English throne in 1272. In 1276 Edward struck into Wales from the north-east, east and south, driving Llywelyn back into the mountainous North West and beginning a ring of encircling castles at Aberystwyth, Builth, Rhuddlan and Flint. This was not the final conflict for in March 1282 the Welsh once again took up arms. By December, however, Llywelyn was dead, killed in a skirmish near Builth Wells. Edward led his troops into North Wales and set about constructing a chain of coastal castles, with accompanying 'planted' towns, that would complete the encirclement of Gwynedd and deter any future uprising.

In planning and executing these great stone fortresses, Edward called on the skills of a remarkable master mason or architect, Master James of St George, whose designs culminated in the classical 'concentric' layout of Harlech and Beaumaris, as well as the final flowering of the 'linear' design at Conwy and Caernarfon, distantly reflecting the two-part layout of the early motte and bailey castles. Although several of the castles remained unfinished, the initial work was carried out at remarkable speed and very great cost, between five and ten million pounds for each castle at present-day values. The details and timetable of construction are in many cases known from contemporary documents. At Harlech, for instance, 1000 men were engaged in the summer of 1285 while more than twice that number were used at Beaumaris ten years later.

While the castles inevitably form the prime focus of attention, the accompanying boroughs, peopled in the first instance by English settlers who often displaced existing Welsh communities, were equally essential to Edward's plan. They, too, survive to a remarkable extent, preserved intact at Caernarfon and Conwy within their imposing town walls. Elsewhere, we have only echoes of their medieval pattern in the street layout of the modern towns. In both cases air photography has no rival in recording the contribution of these medieval foundations to the changing face of Wales.

The royal borough and castle of Caernarfon
When building began at Caernarfon in 1283 the castle and town walls were conceived as a single defensive unit. The great ditch between town and castle was rapidly dug, but the near wall of the castle lagged behind the rest of the circuit. This proved disastrous in 1294 when the Welsh, under Madog ap Llywelyn, took the town and stormed the castle over the half-built wall facing the town; they burned the castle's timber buildings and laid waste the town. But both town and castle were quickly retaken, and building work was resumed, to make the castle the administrative capital of English government that it was always intended to be.

Water played a major part in the defensive scheme, as at most of Edward's castles in Wales. The castle, which required a permanent garrison of only thirty men, had water-gates at either end, and there were originally wet moats outside the town wall and between the castle and town. The Edwardian quay lay within the defensive circuit, just beyond the far end of the castle in this view. The town still retains its medieval street pattern and the town walls are virtually complete, apart from recent gaps for access at lower right and against the now-narrowed line of the castle ditch. The town's twin-towered landward gate can be seen at lower left. A matching gate gave access to the defended foreshore on the opposite side of the town.

Castell Carndochan, Llanuwchllyn, near Bala
Situated on a commanding crag beyond the south-western end of Bala Lake, Castell Carndochan is a typical Welsh castle of the thirteenth century, though it is not mentioned in contemporary records. Seen here in the evening sunshine of April 1994, its tumbled stonework displays at one end the D-shaped tower that so often occurs in the castles of the Welsh princes. At the other end is a circular room or tower, partly built into a natural rock outcrop, while in the centre there stands the remains of a square building or free-standing tower

Castell y Bere, near Tywyn (below)
Deep in the Dysynni valley below Cadair Idris, north-east of Tywyn, Castell y Bere was begun in 1221 by Llywelyn ab Iorwerth ('Llywelyn the Great') to control the southern edge of the kingdom of Gwynedd. Well-built and once splendidly decorated, it has a typically Welsh D-shaped tower at either end, the more distant of the two probably forming a separate keep until joined to the rest of the castle after its fall to the forces of Edward I in 1283. Eleven years later the castle and the small English borough alongside it were attacked and probably burned by the Welsh under Madog ap Llywelyn. Neither town nor castle appears in later records.

Dolwyddelan Castle, near Betws-y-coed (above)
The rectangular keep built by Llywelyn the Great around 1200, and the irregular curtain wall added somewhat later, failed to save Dolwyddelan in January 1283 from Edward I, who then restored the castle for his own use, and added the nearer tower.

Beaumaris Castle, Anglesey

The last and most perfect of Edward's 'concentric' castles is Beaumaris, on the south-eastern shore of Anglesey. Designed by Master James of St George, it was begun in 1295, using a team of 2600 quarrymen, masons and other workers; but the pace of construction soon slowed, and the castle was left unfinished when building work ceased altogether in 1330. The squat towers of its inner ward lack their intended upper storeys and the tall turrets which are such a feature at Caernarfon were not even begun. Beaumaris never saw serious action until attacked and taken by Owain Glyndŵr in 1404. By contrast, the 'planted' town alongside the castle, which supplanted a local Welsh community, grew in its first decade to 132 tenements, probably more than 600 people, and became the main sea-port of North Wales in the Middle Ages. Its protective wall, now largely vanished, was not added until after Glyndŵr's revolt.

Built on an open marshy site, Beaumaris was able to adopt an almost perfect symmetrical design. The castle has a square and massively strong inner ward, with circular towers at each corner, interval towers on two of the walls and bulky twin-towered gatehouses on the other two. The outer ward is delicately hexagonal in shape, and surrounded by a wide moat, now refilled around part of the circuit. Like several of Edward's castles, Beaumaris had direct access to the sea, here through a sea-dock projecting from the near wall; this was originally linked by a short channel to the waters of the Menai Strait.

Slate quarries, copper mines and brickworks

Apart from the winning of gold, copper, lead and other materials, the dominant industry of North West Wales over the past two centuries has been the quarrying of slate, 'the most Welsh of all industries'. The Romans used local slate in their Welsh forts, but large-scale quarrying began only in the late eighteenth century, when new roads replaced previously impassable tracks and the small workings of the Penrhyn estate at Bethesda were drawn into a single organized quarry.

The tripling of the British population in the nineteenth century, and the use of slate in housing and industrial buildings, ensured the prosperity of the quarries (or at least the quarry owners) until almost the end of the century, when over 12,000 quarrymen were employed in North Wales alone. Thereafter, competition from cheaper materials and from imported slate rapidly increased. This, combined with the loss of overseas markets and the effects of the two World Wars, produced a decline which by 1970 had reduced production and manpower to the levels of two centuries earlier.

Although most of the quarries now stand idle, their mark on the landscape of North West Wales is dramatic. The 'big holes' that they created produce stunning images from the air. But aerial recording of the associated slate mills, mining settlements, tramways and docks remains largely a task for the future, before reclamation and reworking obscure the last traces of their original form.

Much of Snowdonia consists of slate, though only limited areas give the consistency of colour and fracture needed for durable roofing slates, the principal output of the North Wales quarries. The two above-ground methods of working - hillside 'galleries' or terraces, like those used at Penrhyn or in the Dinorwic quarries at Llanberis, and the deep 'pit-workings' of the Nantlle Valley, south of Caernarfon - are well represented from the air. It is less easy to do justice to the underground workings that became necessary when the slate-beds were set at an angle to the surface, as around Blaenau Ffestiniog. But even here the vast waste tips are a reminder that every ton of finished slate left up to thirty tons of waste to be disposed of in the surrounding countryside.

However striking the images before him, the air photographer retains a sharp appreciation that the North Wales quarries were made in essence by small teams of four to six men, each working an area or 'bargain' within a quarry, their wages a meagre reward for the skill and resolution that they showed. If the huge gashes in the ground and the glinting grey or purple of the waste tips are a memorial to anyone, it is to these workers of the rock, rather than to the estate owners and the absentee investors who took so much from this once-great industry of North West Wales.

Penrhyn slate quarry, Bethesda (left)
This fine Cambridge University photograph of 1948 shows the towering terraces or 'galleries' into which the quarry was developed from the late eighteenth century onwards. Each originally had its own small finishing sheds, or 'gwaliau', though these were later replaced by vast mechanized processing sheds at lower level, fed by tramways along each gallery and then by inclined plane or cable hoist to the processing area. This is one of the few slate quarries still in operation. Its great rival, the Dinorwic Quarry at Llanberis, closed in 1969, though its magnificent workshops remain open as the Welsh Slate Museum.

Porthmadog and The Cob embankment (right)
Ports, tramways and railways secured the success of the slate quarries. In 1810-11 William Alexander Madocks built the great reclamation embankment now known as The Cob (right foreground); a decade later he developed the harbour at Porthmadog. In 1836 the port was linked to the Ffestiniog Railway; after completion of a tunnel in 1844 trams travelled by gravity all the way from the Ffestiniog quarries to the embankment, and thence by horsepower to the shipping quays in the harbour.

Dorothea slate quarry, Nantlle Valley (left)

Like most quarries in and around the Nantlle Valley, south of Caernarfon, Dorothea was worked by the 'pit' system, its contiguous pits eventually reaching an almost sheer-sided depth of 165 metres. The quarry began work in 1829 and closed in 1970.

The quarry's flooded workings now appear as a single large lake, startlingly blue from the air, with smaller flooded workings alongside. Beyond lies the natural water of Llyn Nantlle Uchaf. The quarry was linked by a tramway, and later a railway, to the 'slate quay' at Caernarfon, now a car park beneath the castle.

Dorothea was one of the few profitable quarries in the Nantlle area, with over 500 workers at its height. It was also unusual in being owned from 1849 by a consortium of local people.

A particular feature is the range of systems for raising slate from the deep pits, notably the massive revetted 'pyramids' that from the turn of the century supported inclined cable hoists. One is visible to the right and another beyond the flooded pit.

At lower right is the tall shed which still houses one of the last Cornish beam-engines, installed to drain the quarry in 1906 and only replaced by electric pumps in 1952. Beyond the right-hand 'pyramid' are the ruins of the quarry's massive nineteenth-century finishing mill.

Gorseddau slate quarry, Treforys village and Ynys-y-pandy mill

The Gorseddau slate quarry, north of Porthmadog, has left splendid remains for the industrial archaeologist. Its very lack of success prevented its early workings from vanishing beneath the waste of later operations. In 1855 a sum of £52,000 was lavished on capital investment, but the slate proved of poor quality and the quarry closed in 1869, never having reached a respectable output.

Top. The quarry's seven main galleries, each with its tip of waste rock to the right. On the left, four of the galleries have been connected by tramways to terraces with dressing sheds, now virtually buried in their own waste. A central inclined plane leads to the head of a tramway which ran all the way to Porthmadog, delivering slate to the finishing mill at Ynys-y-pandy on the way. Near the base of the incline are ruined barracks and a stable block.

Right. The workers' village of Treforys, built by the quarry owners close to the workings at Gorseddau. Eighteen paired dwellings are set out along three streets, with the quarry manager's house sheltered in the trees at top left.

Left. The quarry's three-storey slate mill at Ynys-y-pandy, some distance down the tramway where a stream provided water power. Trams delivered slate along a curved siding to the top floor, and returned them to the main line after sawing and dressing by way of a similarly curved siding from the lowest floor.

Porth-wen brickworks, near Amlwch

This early twentieth-century brickworks on the north coast of Anglesey received silica sand from an adjacent quarry by way of an inclined plane at the left, and exported the finished product from its own quay, which also received incoming fuel for the kilns.

Parys Mountain copper mine and Amlwch Harbour

Right. The 'lunar landscape' of Parys Mountain, in north-east Anglesey, provided one of Britain's richest sources of copper ore from the 1760s until about 1917. Behind the offices of the Mona Mining Company, at lower right, are the vast opencast pits created in the late eighteenth century by collapse and coalescing of earlier underground workings. The ore was processed by roasting and smelting, either on the hill, at the harbour in Amlwch or at Swansea and other export destinations.

Below. Amlwch Harbour. On the right, beyond the stubby pier and small lighthouse that mark the harbour's nineteenth-century entrance, are traces of the kilns, ore- and coal-hoppers which once served the Parys Mountain mine. On the left an early dry-dock now lies hidden behind more recent quays.

98

North East Wales

If it were necessary to name a single landscape which typified North East Wales the choice would probably fall on the fine chain of peaks, crowned by Iron Age hillforts, that make up the Clwydian Range (right), flanked on the east by the mineral-rich limestone plateau of Halkyn Mountain and on the west by the arable and pasture fields of the broad Vale of Clwyd.

The rolling heath and moorland west and south-west of the Vale of Clwyd are in places heavily forested, and marked by natural and artificial lakes for water supply to the towns of the present day. On this inhospitable plateau, exploited in the past only in times of warmer climate, the main traces of past occupation lie in burial mounds of the Bronze Age and the summer steadings, or *hafotai*, of the medieval and post-medieval centuries, forerunners of the modern upland farms. On the moors west of Denbigh both Bronze Age and medieval sites have been excavated and set out for public display during the construction of a reservoir in the Brenig Valley.

Further south the rugged upland and open moors of the Berwyn Range and the high land west of Wrexham, the latter pitted and scarred by mineral workings, are separated from one another by the spectacular valley of the River Dee, opening at the east onto the urban sprawl and partially industrialized landscape west of Wrexham, the largest town of the region. East of Wrexham, Wales extends onto the low land of the Cheshire Plain, incorporating *Maelor Saesneg* (English Maelor), the detached part of Flintshire on pre-1974 maps. Here there is found a distinctive landscape of glacial outwash, peat bogs and meres, ridge and furrow fields, and moated homesteads of the medieval period.

Finally, in the extreme north-east, there are the tidal mudflats of the Dee Estuary and the gently undulating coastal plain, where the mineral resources of Halkyn Mountain and close access to the sea have combined to prompt a degree of industrialization matched elsewhere in the region only around Wrexham.

Here, as in the rest of Wales, the aerial view adds its own perspective to the patterns of past and present in the modern landscape.

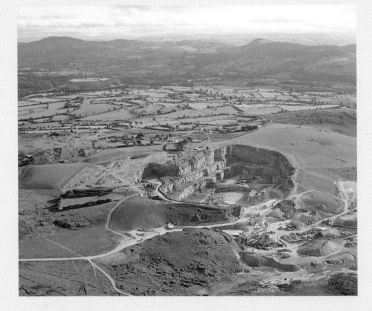

Left. *Castell Dinas Brân and the Dee Valley near Llangollen*
Top right. *Lowland peat at Fenn's Moss, east of Wrexham*
Right. *Halkyn Mountain and the peaks of the Clwydian Range*

From Ice Age to the use of bronze

Capel Garmon chambered tomb, near Betws-y-coed
This Neolithic chambered tomb, with its distinctive wedge-shaped outline and massive capstone, stands close to the Conwy Valley, where the moors of North East Wales give way to the mountains of Snowdonia.

North East Wales has two of the most remarkable early sites in Britain - Bontnewydd Cave, north-west of Denbigh, and the Gop Cairn, above Prestatyn. In addition there is a wealth of burial and ritual monuments from the Bronze Age.

Caves, not surprisingly, are unrewarding subjects for aerial photography. The escarpment and cliffs around the Bontnewydd cave are now heavily wooded, and the surrounding landscape is quite different from the open steppe of 250,000 years ago when the cave, or at least the surrounding area, was used by hunter-gatherers during one of the warmer interludes in the last Ice Age. Excavations at Bontnewydd have produced Palaeolithic hand-axes and other stone tools used by a band of perhaps a dozen men, women and children. Other finds include teeth and bones from an early strain of Neanderthal Man. Finds of this antiquity are extremely rare and the National Museum of Wales continues to explore the Bontnewydd cave for greater understanding of these earliest traces of human occupation in the changing landscape of Wales.

On the limestone plateau above the north-coast resort of Prestatyn stands the Gop Cairn (below), the second-largest artificial mound in Britain, surpassed only by Silbury Hill in Wiltshire. The date and purpose of the cairn remain unknown; a shaft and tunnels dug in the late nineteenth century found no trace of burials within or beneath it. But, bearing in mind the small size of the tunnels and the enormous bulk of the cairn, the failure is neither surprising nor conclusive. Although a Bronze Age date has often been assumed, it is equally likely that the cairn belongs to the preceding Neolithic period, around 2500 BC.

By this time settled farming, perhaps more for the rearing of stock than the growing of crops, was well established in a landscape progressively losing its woodland through man-made clearance. There have been many finds of flint and stone tools but the actual settlements of the time largely elude us. The vast cairn on Gop Hill remains, however, as a powerful reminder of the change from a

Gop Cairn, near Prestatyn
The base of this enormous cairn measures seventy metres by a hundred metres across; its peak, pitted by nineteenth-century diggings, rises fourteen metres above the ridge upon which the cairn stands. On the hillslope in the foreground can be seen the opening to a small rock-shelter or shallow cave. In the nineteenth century excavations uncovered the bones of up to a dozen men and women buried in the cave towards the end of the Neolithic period, about 4500 years ago, in preference to interment in an above-ground tomb like that at Capel Garmon (above).

nomadic 'subsistence' economy to a society in which someone, or some group of people, whether chief or priesthood, could command vast resources of manpower when ritual or symbolism so required.

Viewed from the air, burial and ritual continue to dominate the landscape during the succeeding Early and Middle Bronze Age, from about 2000 to 1000 BC. The exposed but fertile limestone plateau of Halkyn Mountain, to the east of the Clwydian Range, has a dense cluster of Bronze Age round barrows, along with many casual finds of flint tools and metalwork from the period. On the moors to the west and south-west, too, land which had remained largely unoccupied during the Neolithic period saw substantial use in the warmer climate of the Bronze Age, not only for burial and ritual but also for pasture and arable cultivation. This much is suggested by the recovery of cereal pollen from excavated round barrows in the Brenig Valley. Of the farmsteads themselves there is little trace, though the story will be taken up again on later pages.

Earthen circle and barrow at Holywell Racecourse
This large earthen circle, actually an oval up to 100 metres across, has a round barrow set within it, and is joined on the near and far sides by a bank, once thought to be the eighth-century Offa's Dyke. The circle itself has no clear dating evidence, but a Bronze Age or even earlier origin seems possible; it may even be the region's only Neolithic ritual enclosure or 'henge' monument. The massive central grave-pit of the barrow, three metres across and one-and-a-half metres deep, hints that it too may have originated in the Neolithic period, like a recently-excavated barrow further south on the central Borderland near Welshpool.

Ring-ditches in the Tanat Valley

The Tanat Valley, overlooked by the Berwyn Range west of Oswestry, has a gravel subsoil that is ideal for cropmark photography, as seen in a remarkable group of ring-ditches near Llangedwyn, six of them aligned (just left of the house at the centre of the picture) in a way which is common in the Bronze Age barrow cemeteries of southern England but is rarely seen in Wales. Other ring-ditches can be made out at top left and bottom right of the photograph. Also visible, towards the right-hand end of the large central field, is a small penannular cropmark, similar in form to a ritual enclosure of the Middle Neolithic

(dating from about 2800 BC) excavated recently near the timber circle at Welshpool illustrated on page 127. Penannular enclosures of this kind are also known in the Bronze Age. The aligned ring-ditches, and the others nearby, probably represent a Bronze Age barrow cemetery.

Air photography and excavation are beginning to suggest that Neolithic ritual and funerary sites along the northern Borderland may be found more frequently in the valleys, while the barrows of the succeeding Bronze Age occur mainly, but not exclusively, on the higher ground.

Open and enclosed settlements

Domestic settlements from the Bronze Age remain tantalizingly few in Wales. There is little sign of enclosed or defended sites before the latter part of the Bronze Age, and unenclosed settlements would leave little for the archaeologist if built of earth and timber rather than stone. The picture on the right shows one of the few stone settlements of the North East, with at least hints of a Bronze Age origin around 1000 BC.

Soon after this a climatic decline brought about environmental changes that made life in the uplands increasingly precarious, thereby placing pressure on land use and ownership on the lower ground. This, rather than folk-movements, may have prompted construction of the enclosed or defended settlements that dominate the landscape over the next millennium. By around 500 BC many of the impressive hillforts of the North East and other parts of Wales would probably have been in existence, perhaps with a supporting pattern of small farms, fields and managed pasture. An embanked farmstead which may belong to this transitional phase is pictured below, some years after its first discovery from the air.

Open settlement near Cerrigydrudion
These small enclosures and 'wandering walls' at Ffridd Brynhelen, on the Denbigh Moors, may belong to the Bronze Age, though direct dating evidence is lacking. The associated buildings, where they can be made out at all, are small circular or irregular huts. These lie on the edges of the enclosures, not in the centre, suggesting that protection or defence were not primary objectives. Rescue excavations at a nearby settlement, similar in general form to the pattern seen here, suggested occupation around 1000 BC, in the latter part of the Bronze Age.

Enclosed settlement at Cerrigydrudion
This small embanked enclosure at Bryn Têg, on the outskirts of Cerrigydrudion, has traces of five circular building-platforms in its interior, as well as attached field boundaries on falling ground below and to the right of the enclosure, a rare feature in Wales. Preservation of the platforms, on ground which has only gentle slopes, suggests that the site has suffered little if at all from erosion or ploughing. This being so, the enclosing bank may never have been more than an embanked fence or palisade, typical of enclosed sites at the transition from the Bronze Age to the earlier stages of the pre-Roman Iron Age. First discovered during aerial monitoring of scheduled ancient monuments nearby, the settlement is itself now protected as a site of national importance.

What discovery?
Whose discovery?

It is not always clear when, or by whom, an aerial discovery has been made. What matters, above all else, is that the new information should become quickly and widely known after the moment of recognition in the air. Modern record systems and computers are helping to make this possible.

The magnificent view on the left of Caer Drewyn hillfort, near Corwen, still remains unmatched since it was captured in the glancing sunlight of January 1969 by the late Professor J K S St Joseph.

Until then archaeologists knew nothing of the enclosure in the foreground, possibly of Iron Age date, or of the undated field banks and rectangular enclosure on the hillslope beyond. For archaeologists on the Borderland, physically remote from the photographs and card indexes in Cambridge, this remained so for a further fifteen years. Then, in 1984, the sites below the hillfort were 'discovered' again from the air by the regional Archaeological Trust, and added to computerized lists and record-maps then under preparation for all known sites in the region.

Support from readily accessible records, publicly available at both local and national level, is essential if such aerial discoveries are to be speedily shared. The rapid cataloguing of the photographs, and the information they contain, is the first stage in this process, while in Wales a special contribution will soon be made by the development of an Extended National Database (END), pooling the computerized records of the Royal Commission and the four regional Archaeological Trusts.

Caer Drewyn hillfort, Corwen
The hillfort (top) is here seen in January 1969, with Corwen and the Dee Valley beyond. The double-ditched enclosure in the foreground is probably an Iron Age farmstead. The rectangular enclosure and field boundaries on the higher hillslopes are of unknown date.

In recent years the most important discovery for the Roman archaeology of North East Wales came from aerial survey just across the border, at Rhyn Park in Shropshire. There, where the Ceiriog and Dee emerge from the hills west of Chirk, the summer drought of 1975 allowed separate Cambridge University and Manchester University teams to photograph the cropmarks of a previously unsuspected Roman fortress and overlapping smaller fort. The Cambridge photograph on the right, a 'vertical' rather than an 'oblique' view, shows the merit of this kind of photography in giving equal emphasis to all parts of an extensive site, without the distortion of foreground and background inherent in the oblique viewpoint used elsewhere throughout this book.

Interpretation of the fortress, and of the later fort, is still a matter of debate, despite exploratory excavations by Manchester University. It could, perhaps, be an advance base supporting a push into Wales around AD 50, along the ridges west of Chirk. Alternatively, it may have served a more general purpose, housing parts of the Fourteenth Legion and related auxiliaries, on garrison along the Borderland before the creation of their permanent base at Wroxeter, east of Shrewsbury, around AD 55.

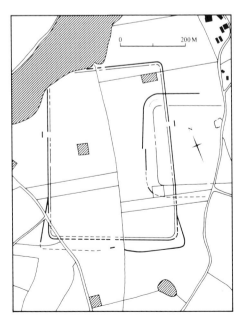

Roman fortress at Rhyn Park, Shropshire

In this vertical photograph, taken by Cambridge University archaeologists shortly after the initial discovery, the fortress, which measures about 500 metres on its longer axis, lies at the centre, with the smaller fort to the right. A short detached length of ditch, or 'titulum', protects the left-hand entrance of the fortress from direct attack. Both a 'titulum' and an offset entrance, like that on the outer ditch of the smaller fort, occur in the cropmark fort near Caersŵs, illustrated on page 140. The Rhyn Park fortress would have held a mixed detachment of legionary troops (Roman citizens) and auxiliaries (non-citizens), numbering at least 5000 men.

A hillfort and its neighbour

The hillfort at Llwyn Bryndinas, Llangedwyn, commands magnificent views along the Tanat Valley, in the foothills of Wales west of Oswestry. Seen here in the summer drought of 1989, its single bank and ditch encircle the hilltop just above the patch of forestry.

Rescue excavations in 1983 showed that the earliest rampart was built, with an impressive facing of stone, around 900 BC. At much the same time, across the Severn Valley to the south-east, a timber-framed rampart was being thrown around the first stage of a massive fort on the Breiddin. The construction of hillforts clearly started on this part of the Borderland in the final centuries of the Bronze Age, before iron came into use for tools and weapons around 700 BC.

The air photograph also includes, below and to the right of the hillfort, a smaller multi-ditched enclosure, first recorded by Cambridge University air photographers in 1960. 'Pairings' of this kind are not uncommon, but without excavation we cannot know whether the hillfort and its neighbour were ever in use together. In this case, as elsewhere, there may have been lengthy periods of abandonment, on one or both sites, during the thousand years from the first hillfort rampart to the radically changed conditions of the Roman period.

Another possibility, attractive but again requiring excavation to test the case, is that the smaller settlement might belong to the centuries *after* the Roman occupation, rather than the native Iron Age *before* it. Air photography is a powerful tool of discovery, but it rarely carries with it unequivocal information about the dating of the sites revealed.

Llwyn Bryndinas hillfort and the neighbouring cropmark enclosure

Dark Age graves

Subtle square cropmarks in a field near Denbigh (right) led to one of the most important Dark Age discoveries in Wales. Although events and folk movements of the post-Roman centuries are known in general terms, the physical traces of daily life, the church and military affairs are depressingly few, particularly so in North East Wales, oscillating as it did between the dominions of the princes of Gwynedd and Powys and the Anglo-Saxon dynasties to the east. Here, as elsewhere, Dark Age researches are likely to follow a halting course, advances coming more by chance than by design.

In this context the square cropmarks at Tandderwen opened up fascinating possibilities. Were they the marks of 'warrior' burials of the pre-Roman Iron Age, like those already known in north-eastern England? Or were they, perhaps, small chapels or burials from the Early Christian era? Or something yet unguessed, new to the region?

Whatever the answer, the imminent subsoiling of the field called for immediate rescue excavation. The field had already been ploughed completely flat, and the subsoiling (to a depth of up to a metre) would rapidly destroy the underground evidence from which the cropmarks grew.

As expected, the ring-ditches proved to mark a Bronze Age cemetery of about 2000 BC, with both inhumation burials and scattered cremations in pits; Bronze Age features are shown in black on the excavation plan on the right. The square ditches, shown in red, were - as half-suspected - part of an Early Christian cemetery, its graves sometimes set within small enclosures, sometimes outside them, in what may well have been family groups.

Unseen in the air photograph, but prominent on the excavation plan, was a much larger square ditch around one of the Bronze Age barrows. Here, perhaps, was a Dark Age burial of particular significance, though the body itself had long since vanished, along with the Bronze Age mound into which it was placed in the sixth or seventh century AD.

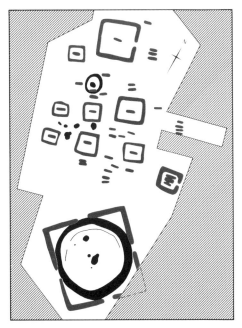

Cropmarks at Tandderwen, Denbigh
At the moment of discovery in 1984 the cemetery caught the writer's eye not for the square cropmarks which later became the main focus of interest but for the ring-ditches of two Bronze Age round barrows, at centre and lower right. Only during later study of the photographs did a smaller square cropmark become apparent beyond the larger ring-ditch. Once the eye had picked this out, it was possible on some of the pictures to identify a smaller square to its left, and indistinct traces of others closer to the camera. An interpretation sketch made at the time proved correct in identifying the presence of these smaller squares, but wrong (and incomplete) in their detailed plotting; only some of the ditches shown on the later excavation plan were detected at this first stage of interpretation. It is common for cropmarks to tell only part of the story in this way, compared with the results of subsequent excavations.

Tandderwen, Denbigh: excavation plan (1:100)
Bronze Age features in black, Dark Age in red. The largest square ditch is about 24 metres across.

Castles of the Welsh and English

In the centuries following the Norman conquest of England the fluctuating power of the Welsh and English left a powerful imprint on North East Wales. As in the preceding Dark Age, this remained a disputed and unstable border zone. Like other parts of Wales it owes much of its finest military architecture to Edward I and his leading baronial followers in the campaigns of 1276-77 and 1282-83, though the Welsh princes built their own castles, as at Tomen y Rhodwydd (below) and Castell Dinas Brân (page 113).

On the facing page is the magnificent English castle and walled town of Denbigh, begun under Edward's protection in 1282 and now largely cleared of post-medieval clutter to improve access and visibility for visitors. Of Edward's own works, effected through his military architect, Master James of St George, Rhuddlan Castle (over the page) is one of the finest.

Also pictured on the next few pages are the baronial castles at Chirk and Ruthin, their military attributes here softened by the gardens and landscaping of more recent times. Finally, on page 145, the aerial perspective captures the classical simplicity of the motte and bailey castle at Sycharth, where Owain Glyndŵr's timber hall was put to flames in 1403, in the early days of the last Welsh uprising.

The castle and walled town of Denbigh (right)
Denbigh Castle, begun in 1282 by Henry de Lacy, earl of Lincoln, crowns an isolated hilltop on the western edge of the Vale of Clwyd. Its massive triple-towered gatehouse is unique. On the slopes outside the castle stood the thirteenth-century town, its protective wall still curving round from the right to the twin towers of the Burgess Gate, before passing out of the picture on the left and striking back up the hill to regain the castle. Within the medieval town, now sparsely populated, stand the isolated tower of St Hilary's church, dating from about 1300, and the gaunt colonnades of the Earl of Leicester's unfinished church, begun in 1578 in a failed attempt to supplant the cathedral church of St Asaph. The High Street of modern Denbigh, in the foreground, grew from fourteenth-century and later settlement outside the medieval walls. The large building blocking the street's left-hand end is the Shire Hall of 1572, much altered in 1780. Beyond the town rise the towers and gables of the North Wales Counties Lunatic Asylum (later the Denbigh Hospital), built by subscription in 1848 as one of the first products of the Lunacy Act of 1845.

Tomen y Rhodwydd motte and bailey, near Ruthin
Close beside the A525 trunk road from Wrexham to Ruthin and Corwen, Tomen y Rhodwydd (also known as Castell y Rhodwydd) is one of the finest motte and bailey castles in Wales. Historical references suggest that it was built in 1149 by Owain ap Gruffydd (Owain Gwynedd), prince of Gwynedd. The castle makes no further appearance in contemporary documents and its later history is unknown.

Rhuddlan: a Saxon, Norman and Edwardian town

Rhuddlan boasts one of Edward I's finest castles, its high-towered and battlemented inner ward standing within a lower and deeply-moated outer line of defence. Built between 1277 and 1282, it was given navigable access to the coast through a vast civil engineering scheme which canalized the formerly meandering course of the River Clwyd into a new and deeper channel, largely followed to the present day (smaller photo).

The Rhuddlan of today is the fourth town on the site. First came the Anglo-Saxon town of Cledemutha ('Clwyd-mouth'), founded by Edward the Elder in AD 921; it is possible that this lay largely south of the modern town, stretching into the foreground in the smaller view. Alternatively, it may have occupied much the same area as its Norman successor, alongside the imposing motte and bailey castle known as Twt Hill, seen at lower right in the larger photo. Thirdly, at upper left in the same view, came the castle and embanked town of Edward I, extending further to the north. The sequence is completed by the post-medieval and modern town, spreading more widely again to the east and north.

Excavations at Rhuddlan have also produced finds of Roman material, as well as scatters of worked flint from the Mesolithic period, around 7000-4000 BC.

Llangollen and Castell Dinas Brân

Two memorable sights for visitors to the International Eisteddfod at Llangollen are the silhouette of Castell Dinas Brân, just east of the town, and the sweeping limestone cliffs of Eglwyseg Rocks. The larger aerial view brings the two together in a new and dramatic perspective, emphasizing the curving defences of the pre-Roman hillfort within which the castle was built for one of the princes of Powys by about 1270. Once magnificently decorated, and with a strong square keep at its eastern end, this unusual rectangular castle was burned and abandoned in 1277 in the face of Edward I's advance. It was never rebuilt, and has suffered much from later stone-robbing.

In the smaller picture the town of Llangollen lines the banks of the River Dee, linked by a fine stone bridge of about 1500. The engine sheds and rolling-stock of the steam-powered and now-revived Vale of Llangollen Railway curve round at centre right, while another nineteenth-century artery of communication, the Shropshire Union Canal, snakes along higher ground, just to the left of the Eisteddfod's white-roofed pavilion.

Castle into house and garden

Not all castles fell gracefully or suddenly into obscurity when their military usefulness was over. Some found new life as houses of the nobility. Importance and wealth, of family or class, were expressed in grand buildings, a fine life-style and (increasingly from the sixteenth century) the pleasures of the garden as a setting for the house and its social events. The tiny gardens created for Queen Eleanor at each of Edward I's great fortresses in North Wales - Rhuddlan, Conwy and Caernarfon - thus find an echo centuries later in the landscaped setting of Ruthin Castle (opposite) and the formal terrace and wooded backdrop of Chirk Castle (left).

From the air, indeed, it is often the gardens or landscaped settings that predominate, especially in the great houses of the seventeenth century and later. This is very clear at Erddig Park (below), where it is the restored formal gardens that catch the eye, not the simple geometry of the house and service yards in the background.

Chirk Castle and its formal garden (above)
The squat towers of Chirk Castle betray a building unfinished or partially demolished after its late thirteenth-century beginnings, while the many windows reflect unbroken use as a residence and stately home since its military significance was lost. The original south front, in the background, would have had two more corner towers and perhaps a twin-towered gatehouse, but may never have been built. Its place is now taken by the castle's fifteenth- and sixteenth-century domestic quarters and chapel, and by later service buildings. The clipped yews of the reinstated formal garden lie to the left of the castle, now managed by the National Trust and set in landscaped parkland of the eighteenth century.

Restored gardens at Erddig Park, Wrexham (left)
This red-brick mansion of 1683-1733 has been meticulously restored by the National Trust, and the gardens recreated in their eighteenth-century design.

Ruthin Castle and its gardens (right)
It was a land dispute with the owner of Ruthin Castle that sparked Owain Glyndŵr's rebellion in 1400. Begun after Edward I's campaign of 1276-77, the castle retains only parts of its curtain wall and some of its internal towers - two can be clearly seen in this view. The rest of the buildings belong to a castellated mansion of the early nineteenth century, and to the castle's use as a nursing home from 1922. It is now a prestigious hotel. In their present form the gardens date mainly from the nineteenth century. In a field beyond the castle stand the stones of the bardic circle of the National Eisteddfod of 1873.

Lowland and wetland

'English Maelor', or *Maelor Saesneg*, where Wales projects into England south-east of Wrexham, owes its distinctive landscape not only to geology and the nature of its soils but also to a history of settlement and land use that is very different from that of most of Wales.

Low-lying and seemingly flat from the air - *maelor* means simply 'plain' or 'lowland' - the area is transformed under low sunlight into a landscape of humps and bumps, marked by the sinuous ridges and hillocks of glacial outwash onto the Cheshire Plain. At Hanmer (left), and around Ellesmere in Shropshire, there is a minor lake district of open-water 'meres' and peat-filled 'mosses' that were created by the melting of the Welsh and Irish ice-mass 10,000 years ago.

Lowland bogs like Fenn's Moss (below left) are rare features in the modern landscape, most having suffered severely from drainage and peat-cutting. They have a special value for archaeologists in preserving pollen and plant debris which can tell the story of environmental change and the impact of man in the millennia since the last retreat of the ice.

Maelor has few traces of pre-medieval settlement; the area may have been heavily wooded until quite a late date, though clearance must have taken some effect by the Roman period. In the post-Roman centuries the area was held by the princes of Powys, and

Hanmer Mere (top left) ***and Fenn's Moss*** (left)
Two pictures of characteristic Maelor landscapes.

In the upper photograph, curving ridge and furrow fields, which underlie the tents of a Scout camp to the left of the lake, clearly pre-date the carefully contrived landscape of Gredington Park. To the right of the Mere the water-side slopes are marked by straighter ridge and furrow ploughing, which may be more recent in date.

In the lower photograph the tree-lined Shropshire Union Canal, first opened in 1805 as the Ellesmere Canal, cuts across Fenn's Moss close to the border with Shropshire. The geometrical pattern in the foreground is the result of peat-cutting. Commercial peat-cutting in Fenn's Moss has only recently ceased.

less frequently by the princes of Gwynedd. By the eighth century, however, it had fallen - more or less - under the control of the Anglo-Saxon kings of Mercia, builders of the great dykes along its western edge (shown in the pictures on pages 142-3).

It was only in the Middle Ages and later, however, that Maelor acquired the most distinctive features of its historic landscape, the moated sites illustrated on page 118, and the pervading ridge and furrow cultivation (opposite) used to tame the district's fertile but heavy soils. From early in the nineteenth century the landscape largely reverted to dairy pasture, 'sweetened' at first from marl pits dug in the fields themselves and more recently by chemical fertilisers and periodic ploughing for cereals, root-crops and (most recently) the yellow-flowering oilseed rape.

Nowhere else in Wales is a landscape of ridge and furrow cultivation preserved on the scale seen here. Even so, vast tracts have already been flattened by modern ploughing. Paradoxically, the loss may be partly balanced for the air photographer by the cropmark and soilmark evidence which then emerges for the underlying archaeology of earlier periods. The area will need much more attention, however, before it matches the results that have so enhanced our picture of settlement further south on the Borderland (pages 19 and 135).

Ridge and furrow fields at Bowen's Hall, Hanmer
Ridge and furrow field systems, often showing several phases of development, may date from any time between the Middle Ages and the nineteenth century, or even later. Here, the 'horizontal' ridges at centre right have a plain strip or 'headland' at either end where the plough turned before commencing the next furrow. These ridges overlie and obscure 'vertical' ridging at the far end of the field, though the earlier pattern is only lightly scored where the two meet. To the left, gently curving furrows are interrupted by later cross-ploughing, and by the sunken area of an abandoned marl pit, which once provided alkaline material to 'sweeten' the acidic surface clays. Other pits lie close to the farm and at the field boundary in the far distance.

Moated homesteads

For the aerial archaeologist moated sites, almost always square or rectangular in shape, are a distinctive feature of the Maelor landscape, a westerly extension of the English manorial system of the twelfth to fourteenth centuries. They are also common in the anglicized parts of South Wales. Built as the residences of minor lords and their stewards, or estate managers, they continued in use as homes of the landed gentry. A few moats have known or suspected ecclesiastical connections, as the seats of bishops or parsons, or the centres of monastic granges. Others may have been moated dovecotes or rickyards, some perhaps of relatively recent date.

The high concentration of moats in central Maelor - over twenty are known and others no doubt await discovery - has been interpreted as the result of penetration by settlers, from around AD 1300, into areas of waste or heavy woodland, though this has yet to be tested by excavation. Under excavation, moated sites can offer special insights into everyday aspects of medieval life. Their central 'islands', often untouched by later occupation or cultivation, may preserve traces of the masonry or half-timbered buildings that once stood upon them, while their waterlogged moats may hold crop remains, foodstuffs and wood or leather that would long since have decayed on dry-land sites.

Three homestead moats near Hanmer
Top. *At Peartree Lane a well-preserved moat stands in a field called 'chapel garth', a name which suggests some kind of ecclesiastical connection.*
Left. *At Halghton Lodge the moat has been all but consumed by later ridge and furrow ploughing.*
Below. *At Bryn a previously unknown moat near a field called 'moat meadow' is seen at the moment of rediscovery in the glancing sunlight of a winter's afternoon.*

Industry and mineral extraction

The rich and varied mineral resources of North East Wales are concentrated in a band of Carboniferous Limestone and Coal Measures which underlie the Flintshire Plateau, alongside the Dee Estuary, and which then stretch southward to the foothills west of Wrexham.

The accessibility of the Flintshire lead ores attracted workings in the Roman period, not least for the ease of export by sea from the Dee Estuary; mines in the area were also active during the great era of castle-building in the thirteenth and early fourteenth centuries. From this time, and perhaps even from as early as the Roman period, small shafts proliferated on Halkyn Mountain and other parts of the Flint-shire Plateau, while another set of workings developed around Minera, west of Wrexham. Later, zinc-blende too was heavily exploited, though both industries declined rapidly from the beginning of the twentieth century, despite strenuous efforts over the previous hundred years to provide adequate drainage for the ever-deeper mines of the Flintshire leadfield.

The presence of iron ore, close to ready supplies of timber and (from the 1720s) coking coal, led to a thriving iron industry west of Wrexham, focussed for forty years from 1753 on the cannon works and general foundry which Isaac and John Wilkinson established on the

Lead-mining on Halkyn Mountain, near Flint. *Lines of mounds, each surrounding a shaft, indicate workings on parallel lodes of lead ore.*

western edge of Wrexham at Bersham, where iron production first began in the 1670s. The Bersham works provided cylinders for the early steam-engines of Boulton and Watt, but a family feud in 1793 led to a decline and to the transfer of activity to Brymbo, a little further north. In 1884 Brymbo produced the first steel to be made in Britain by the open-hearth process, and expansion continued into the twentieth century, not least through development of the vast John Summers steelworks at Shotton, on Deeside, once employing several thousand workers but reduced since the 1980s to only minor operations. With the closure in 1990 of the steelworks at Brymbo, steelmaking in the region has been virtually extinguished, like coalmining before it, only the Point of Ayr colliery in the far north-east now remaining open.

For many centuries the region's rich limestone deposits have been worked for building stone, but the Industrial Revolution brought new uses. Iron and steel production called for limestone as a flux in the smelting process, while increasingly intensive arable cultivation demanded lime for the fields. More recently, road construction has taken vast quantities of stone from the region's many quarries, both for aggregates and for coated tarmacadam for surfacing work. From the air the white and yellow gashes of the limestone quarries, against the green of the rural landscape, have a strange fascination, rarely matched, unfortunately, by close inspection on the ground.

Two other industries deserve mention here. First, chemical production, which has thrived both on the Dee Estuary and at Acrefair, south-west of Wrexham, where production started soon after the middle of the nineteenth century. Secondly, the manufacture of brick and tile in the Ruabon area, where the local red marl has been used to produce terracotta and an almost indestructible red brick that has left its distinctive mark on housing and municipal buildings along the whole of the northern Borderland.

Chemical works at Acrefair, near Wrexham

At Acrefair, alongside the Dee south of Wrexham, Robert Ferdinand Graesser began making paraffin from colliery waste in 1867; he later produced phenol, synthetic dyes and picric acid. From 1928 Monsanto Chemicals have made products here for the textile, pharmaceutical and food industries. The plant is now the main European manufacturing centre for Monsanto's specialized industrial chemicals. Between the works and the distant Shropshire Plain can be seen the viaduct which carried the Shrewsbury & Chester Railway of 1846-47, and later the GWR, across the River Dee at Newbridge.

Hafod Tileries, Ruabon

This 1984 picture catches Henry Dennis's tileworks of 1878 in a state of transition. The 'beehive' kilns in the centre, with extrusion and drying sheds on the left, were already awaiting demolition in favour of a new tunnel-kiln in the building on the right. Dennis Ruabon Ltd are still the largest makers of quarry tiles in the United Kingdom.

Minera limestone quarry, near Wrexham (right)

First worked on a large scale in the nineteenth century, the Minera Quarry produced aggregates and surfacing materials for road construction until its recent closure. In this 1990 view freshly quarried stone (upper left) has been brought to a crushing and coating plant (centre), while stores of prepared materials occupy other parts of the quarry floor. Just out of sight in the foreground is the survivor of two brick-built Hoffman kilns which were used from about 1868 until the late 1920s to make lime for agriculture and the building industry. Disused lead-workings, some of them dating back to the sixteenth century or earlier, lie just out of frame to the right. Conifer plantations like the one in the background have transformed much of the region's higher land in the past forty years.

The Brenig archaeological trail

In the 1970s the Brenig Valley, between Denbigh and Cerrigydrudion, was the scene of major rescue excavations in advance of work on Llyn Brenig, one of several man-made lakes which, along with vast tracts of conifer plantation, have transformed the Denbigh Moors in recent years. The excavations focussed on a group of Bronze Age barrows and ritual monuments but also explored the Mesolithic, Iron Age and later use of the valley, including the walls and enclosures of a medieval *hafod* or summer settlement, shown on the facing page. From the outset it was an objective of the project to restore the monuments that lay above the intended water-line to form an 'archaeological trail' around the fringes of the lake. Shown here in the snowy winter of 1986, the trail is now linked to a far-sighted scheme of landscape and wildlife interpretation, explained through a lakeside exhibition centre developed by Welsh Water/Dŵr Cymru on the B4501 road from Cerrigydrudion to Denbigh.

Bronze Age ring-cairn and round barrow, with ice on Llyn Brenig

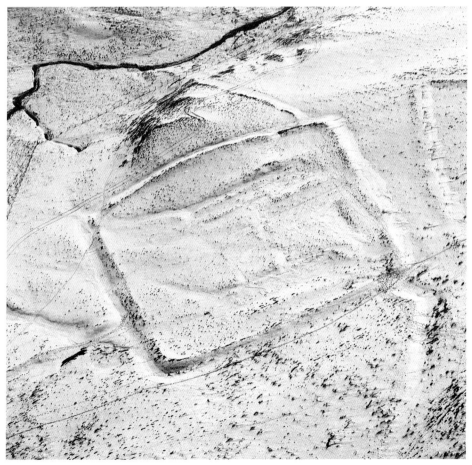

Hen Ddinbych: a monastic grange? (left)
The embanked enclosure known as Hen Ddinbych ('old Denbigh') stands in a secluded position on the eastern side of the Brenig Valley. Its origins remain a mystery, though the 1334 'Survey of the Honour of Denbigh' suggests a possible solution. It refers to

> ... *a certain waste called Bysshopeswall, which contains 1127 acres .... with the hamlet of Bere-bowe and Havothlum adjoining, the pasture of which is sold annually to the community for 20 shillings ...*

Hafod-lom is a nearby farm and the Berbo a local stream, so a link with Hen Ddinbych seems highly probable. If so, the name 'Bishopswall' hints at an ecclesiastical connection, as does local usage of 'hen eglwys' (the old church) for the long building whose stone-robbed footings lie near the far side of the enclosure. Hen Ddinbych might, therefore, be a monastic grange, or upland farm, belonging to Denbigh Priory or another of the religious houses of North East Wales. It was presumably not a success, since by 1334 its pasture had been leased to the local community. Whatever its origins, Hen Ddin-bych now stands as one of the attractions of the Brenig archaeological trail.

'Hafod' settlement alongside Llyn Brenig (right)
Trails of footprints link the rectangular walls and curving banks of a summer steading near the head of the lake. The settlement produced pottery and metalwork of the fifteenth to sixteenth centuries. A ring of posts at centre left marks the place where a timber roundhouse was built at a much earlier date, probably in the pre-Roman Iron Age.

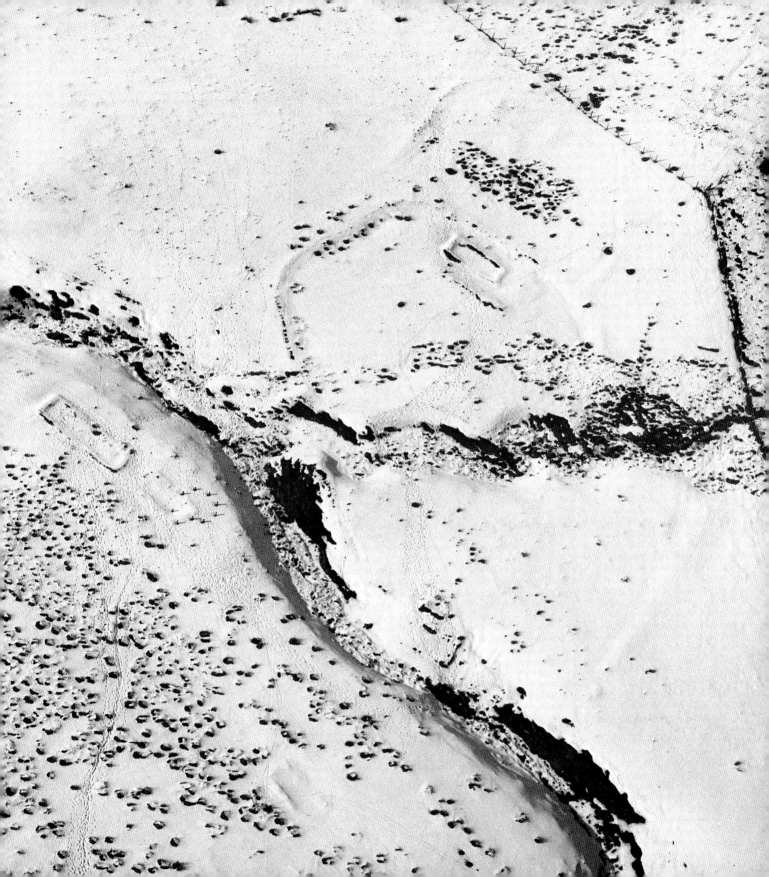

The Border landscape, from Llanddewi Ystradenni, north of Llandrindod Wells, to the Black Mountains of South East Wales

Central Wales and the Borderland

Sea and coast have meant much to the regions visited so far, but we now turn to the land-locked uplands of central Wales and the more broken scenery of the eastern Borderland.

The inhospitable 'spine' of the Cambrian Mountains is in essence a deeply dissected upland plateau, heavily moulded by ice, wind and rain. Its landscape of bare or bracken-covered slopes gives way to bleak stretches of coarse grass or heather upland, rooted in blanket peat or in heavily acidified soils which support no livestock beyond hardy mountain sheep. Conifer plantations and catchment reservoirs have left their mark on the higher land, as has pasture improvement in recent years. The scattered farms of the deeply-cut valleys, mostly glacial in origin, sit amongst small fields outlined by hedges rather than stone-built walls. There is virtually no arable cultivation and only a small contribution from beef and dairy farming.

To the east, the scenery of the Borderland is altogether more varied, the high land dropping steeply to the Midland Plain around Wrexham but giving way along the Upper Severn Valley to low and close-set ridges which from the air give the landscape a distinctive 'grain' from south-west to north-east. Beyond the Severn Valley the high land spreads into south-west Shropshire, and reaches right up to the border along the deeply indented junction with the Herefordshire plain. Further south again the broadening valley of the River Wye faces the steep northern bluff of the Monmouthshire Black Mountains, beyond which lies the lower land of South East Wales, where this aerial journey began.

The Borderland shows little sign of industry, a regular scattering of small market towns serving a rural economy based on beef and dairy farming, with sheep on the higher ground and a small amount of arable cultivation in the Upper Severn Valley and along the border with Herefordshire.

Predictably, the central uplands have thinly scattered but often well-preserved traces of man's past, though recent work shows that much is still to be discovered through field survey and air photography. By contrast, the Borderland, a zone of conflict throughout history and prehistory, has a richness and diversity that equals anything else in Wales.

The commanding hillforts of the Iron Age, the matching lowland settlements first discovered from the air, the camps and forts of the Roman army, Offa's great boundary dyke stretching 'from sea to sea', and the earth and timber castles of the Marcher lords - all these are featured on the following pages. Along with traces of agricultural communities from the earliest times to the last century, these pictures bring our aerial tour of Wales to a fittingly varied close.

Upland peat bog at Waun Fignen Felen, Fforest Fawr (top right)
An eroding peat bog in an area used by Mesolithic hunters around 7000 years ago.

Pontsticill Reservoir, Brecon Beacons (right)
A reservoir constructed in the 1920s to serve the needs of the capital city, Cardiff.

Ritual and burial on the Borderland

At Sarn-y-bryn-caled, on the flood-plain of the River Severn just south of Welshpool, several years of air photography have revealed an important ritual and funerary complex of the Neolithic and early Bronze Age, none of it visible above ground. The ritual enclosure or *henge* shown on page 12 lies a few kilometres to the south.

The first discoveries were made by Cambridge University photographers in July 1969, when two long parallel cropmarks (left), thought to be the ditches of a Neolithic ritual avenue or *cursus*, were seen as darker marks in the parched grassland and ripening corn. Beyond the far end of the cursus, and slightly to its left, lay a large and a small ring-ditch, also likely to be ritual or funerary monuments of the Neolithic or Bronze Age.

In the long hot summer of 1975 the Cambridge University photographers again recorded the ditches of the cursus (below), and this time added nearby a remarkable circle of twenty pits or post-holes ranged around a central mark that seemed likely to represent an enormous pit.

In later years the Clwyd-Powys Archaeological Trust, which is based at Welshpool, photographed further circular and penannular ditches in the nearby fields, gradually uncovering one of the largest and most varied groupings of ritual and funerary sites yet known in Wales.

Ritual avenue and timber circle at Welshpool
Above. *The cropmarks of the ritual avenue in 1969.*
Right. *Six years later the pits of the timber circle appear on the near side of the road, with the northern end of the cursus beyond at upper left.*

In 1990-91 construction of a relief road round Welshpool prompted excavation of several of the sites, notably the pit-circle, which now lies beneath the southern end of the new bypass. Trial trenches across the cursus showed the central avenue to have been about ten metres wide, with parallel banks outside its flanking ditches; charcoal from low in the ditches suggested construction in about 3800 BC. A small penannular enclosure to the east, equipped with entrance posts and with cremations in the terminals of its two-phase ditch, had been dug in about 3000 BC, while the larger of two heavily eroded ring-ditches, 500 metres to the north, was cut in about 2000 BC during the early stages of the Bronze Age. The pit-circle itself was fully excavated (right) and proved to have been a double timber circle, built in about 2100 BC; timber circles are often associated with 'henge' monuments, of which Stonehenge is our best-known but least typical example.

Here, at Welshpool, the discovery from the air of a group of sites virtually lost to ploughing has been carried through to a planned programme of rescue excavation. Between them, the two archaeological techniques have told us something of the growth and use of an important ritual complex, a focus of activity over almost 2000 years for early farming communities on the Borderland of Wales.

Timber circle at Welshpool

Above, the circle is shown near the end of excavation early in 1991. It measured just under eighteen metres across and consisted of a ring of twenty stout oak timbers, with two larger posts forming an 'entrance' at the south. A large central cropmark on the air photograph resolved itself into an inner setting of six even larger posts, burned in position. These in turn enclosed two successive cremation burials, the earlier including burned flint arrowheads that hinted at ritual sacrifice. Alongside the inner posts a massive oak log, a metre in diameter, had been split and set upright at either end of a dark-stained hollow, perhaps to support some kind of altar or ritual table for the laying out of a corpse, or alternatively to provide a 'porch' and entrance threshold to the central area. Radiocarbon samples from several parts of the circle indicated construction in about 2100 BC, at the transition from the Neolithic period to the Early Bronze Age. The picture on the left shows the circle reconstructed experimentally after the end of the 1991 excavations.

The photograph of the excavated timber circle has been provided by the Clwyd-Powys Archaeological Trust, as have many of the air photographs in the introduction and in this and the previous section of the book.

Above. *July 1984, west end*

Above. *July 1986, centre.* Below. *July 1984, east end*

The last two pages have shown the emergence of a *group* of sites over several years of air photography. This page tells a similar story for a *single* site at Walton Green, near the border with Herefordshire, east of New Radnor.

In the long dry summer of 1984 (top) overlapping cropmarks revealed two rectangular enclosures, the longer one 'disappearing' at the left into a field of ripened crop, where no marks showed. Two years later, in July 1986, the original marks were missing (centre) but two parallel lines of cropmarks, about thirty metres apart, continued across the full width of the next two fields, before again vanishing into an unresponsive crop. In 1989 the whole length of the marks, now stretching 400 metres or more, was recorded in a series of colour photographs, and there were faint hints of a continuation in a field further east again.

It was only during work for this book, however, that the final piece of the jigsaw fell into place, showing the marks to belong to a Neolithic *cursus* or avenue like that at Welshpool, already seen on page 126. In 1984 a single colour slide (bottom left) had recorded a fragment of cropmark ditch, with a sharply rounded corner, at a road junction some way east of Walton Green. At first sight this looked like the corner of a small Roman practice camp, like those illustrated on page 86, and it was classified as such on the local archaeological record. But in 1993, when this little segment of ditch was plotted along with the other cropmarks, it fell exactly on the line of the conjectured cursus (top right in the drawing below), providing a squared end at the east to match that already seen over 660 metres away to the west.

The story of this rare and important discovery is an object lesson in the need to photograph even small traces of cropmarks, year after year, and to plot the information regularly onto large-scale maps, so that each piece of information can be seen, and reinterpreted if need be, in relation to its neighbours.

Ritual avenue at Walton Green, near New Radnor

Left. *Separate sections of the avenue as seen from the air in 1984 and 1986.*
Below. *A known round barrow (at the west, black hachures), the newly-discovered cursus (red), and three overlapping cropmark enclosures (blue) sketch-plotted at a scale of 1:10,000 against the local field and road boundaries.*

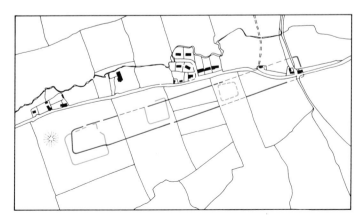

Bronze Age commemorative and burial cairns, dating from about 2000-1200 BC, often occupy prominent ridges or hilltops, two of the most spectacular standing on the peaks of Pen y Fan and Corn Du in the Brecon Beacons (above). Unfortunately both had begun to suffer in recent years from the feet and hands of the thousands of walkers who now make their way up the ridge-top footpaths to gaze over the dramatic glacial *cwms* scooped into the northern face of the Beacons.

Only rescue excavation could save the remnants of the cairns, and this was carried out in 1991 and 1992 before both were rebuilt in more durable form. The smaller picture shows work in progress on the Corn Du cairn, with its long-robbed central burial cist and the surrounding stone kerbs clearly visible against the underlying peat. Similar peat, which began to cover large parts of upland Wales some time before 2000 BC, appears in the foreground of the larger photograph. The surface beneath the cairn, when first uncovered, had grass as green as the day it was buried, around 4000 years ago, along with beetles and pollen giving clues to the environmental conditions of the time.

The Brecon Beacons (above) *and the Corn Du cairn under excavation* (below)

Iron Age hillfort at Cefncarnedd, near Caersŵs

The hillfort looks down from a narrow ridge onto the fertile triangle of low land later used by the Romans for their forts at Caersŵs (pages 138, 140). Like many Borderland hillforts it underwent major changes and expansion during its lifetime. The earliest fort occupies the right-hand end of the ridge, its flattened double bank cutting across the ridge about half-way along. Later the defences were extended farther to the left, where a simple entrance gave access through strong double banks. A less prominent third rampart may be a still-later addition, perhaps along with a bank striking downslope towards the camera and then to the right to form an outer enclosure or annexe. Common in Borderland hillforts, such outer enclosures may have been used for the seasonal corralling of stock or for protected grazing in times of danger. A final phase of use, perhaps even in the post-Roman centuries, is marked by an unusually well-preserved bank subdividing the central area near the right-hand end of the hill.

Pen-y-gaer hillfort, Llanwyddelan, near Welshpool

Late summer sunshine strikes across the single bank and ditch of a much smaller fort in the hill-country south-west of Welshpool. The topography of low parallel ridges and the pattern of irregular hedged fields are typical of this part of the Borderland.

The Iron Age on the Borderland

The Cambrian Mountains have only a thin scattering of Iron Age hillforts. The Borderland, by contrast, has a density unrivalled anywhere else in Britain, with more than 100 major forts and perhaps twice as many smaller ones between the Severn Estuary and the North Wales coast. The variety of shape, size and defensive pattern suggests a long period of development and change over the 1000 years or so from the final stages of the Bronze Age to the Roman Conquest in the first century AD. Within this period neighbouring forts may have been occupied at quite different times, as each began life, flourished or fell into abandonment and decay.

The forts may also have varied in function, both in time and space. The larger ones no doubt combined a variety of roles, largely hidden from us today. Some, if not all, may have protected - and expressed - the power of local chieftains, while at the same time acting as centres of trade or craft activity, or as storage and redistribution points for foodstuffs and other kinds of communal wealth.

Thirty years ago, on the basis of the surviving sites alone, this looked like a pattern of heavily defended settlements or strongholds in an otherwise 'empty' landscape, the fertile lower slopes and valley floors perhaps choked by swamp and forest in the centuries before the Roman conquest.

In the Upper Severn Valley, however, there were enough enclosures of similar type on the hillslopes and lower ground to suggest that this view might be incomplete. It was air photography, or rather aerial exploration, that strikingly proved this to be so.

The area has soils and geology that broadly favour the development of cropmarks in the summer months, and there is enough arable cultivation to bring substantial parts of the landscape into play for the aerial archaeologist at this time. The amount of cultivated land falls sharply to the west, however, where even lowland fields come under the plough only sporadically, so that many years of work are required before the photographer can give any assurance that a reasonable part of the landscape has been seen in suitable conditions for cropmark recording. Once or twice each decade severe drought produces cropmarks in the grass of the pasture fields and uncultivated hillslopes, where they are rarely seen in normal summers.

Over the five decades since the first Cambridge University flights into the area after the Second World War, cropmark photography of hillslope and lowland areas, heavily eroded by ploughing from the Roman period onwards, has produced large numbers of previously unknown cropmark enclosures, as well as many archaeological sites of other

Penycastell hillfort, Llangyniew, near Welshpool
This small fort on a rounded hilltop west of Welshpool has up to five lines of defence, with a gradually narrowing entranceway at lower right.

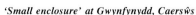
'Small enclosure' at Gwynfynydd, Caersŵs
Ancient and modern farmsteads sit alongside one another on gently sloping land above the flood plain of the River Severn.

'Small enclosure' at Varchoel Lane, Guilsfield, near Welshpool
This multi-ditched enclosure sits on the valley floor north of Welshpool. The cropmarks also include an overlapping trackway and an ill-defined ring-ditch in the foreground, which may belong to a ploughed-out Bronze Age barrow.

Iron Age farmstead at Collfryn, near Welshpool
Below. *The cropmarks of a hillslope enclosure north of Welshpool can still be seen as rescue excavations begin in the face of plough-erosion. Slight earthworks in the right-hand field include a sunken entrance track.*
Right. *At a later stage the excavations have revealed the drainage ditches of timber roundhouses and the postholes of other structures. The farmstead began life around 300 BC and lasted, in modified form, into the Roman period.*

kinds (page 19). The enclosures vary widely in size and form, and - like the hillforts - not all would have been in use at the same time or necessarily for the same purpose. But the increase in information available for discussion and explanation is remarkable. There is little sign, either, that the pace of discovery is slowing, and the search is now extending into areas which were not so intensively examined in previous years.

The dating and function of these newly discovered sites is not in itself revealed by the cropmark evidence. Archaeologists can only speculate, from similarities of form, that some of them belong to broadly the same landscape as the embanked and ditched hillforts on the hilltops and higher slopes. Even the hillforts, in the last resort, are only dated by analogy with the few of their number that have produced datable material from excavation or the collection of surface finds.

Apart from continuing aerial survey, and mapping of the results for comparative analysis, an obvious next step in the study of this material was to construct a planned programme of field survey and excavation, to search out similarities or differences of siting, form or relationship and to tie these if possible to specific parts of the Iron Age or the native Roman period.

Such a programme would look at a variety of questions. Does the siting and relationship of enclosures tell us anything about their date or function? Do rectangular sites on hillslopes, for instance, differ from curvilinear ones on the valley floor? Can different varieties of rectangular or curvilinear sites be identified, perhaps from the sharpness of their corners or some other quirk of design? Do rectangular enclosures

Cropmark enclosure at Cloddiau, near Montgomery

It was the place-name, Welsh for 'banks', that first attracted archaeologists to this site in the late 1970s. The location, on a hillock set slightly apart from higher ground, seemed entirely appropriate for an Iron Age farmstead. Ground visits and watching from the air added nothing, however, until parching of the grass in 1989 produced the unmistakable cropmarks of a double-ditched enclosure encircling the hilltop. In the foreground the clearly-marked entrance is fronted by a ditch running downslope and swinging right to form an attached field system or 'annexe', perhaps returning to meet a third enclosure ditch visible beyond the farm buildings. The timing of the flight was fortunate: within a couple of days the newly-arrived cattle would have eaten the lusher grass of the cropmarks and left the hilltop as featureless as the well-grazed field at top right.

Cropmarks at Great Cloddiau, near Newtown

The cropmarks of a double-ditched rectangular enclosure lie only a field away from the surviving earthworks of an Iron Age hillfort, hidden in an oval of trees. It seems barely credible that the two could have been in use at the same time. The form of the hillfort suggests that it probably dates from the earlier part of the Iron Age. If so, the cropmarks might represent a farmstead that came into use later in the pre-Roman period, after the hillfort had been abandoned. Alternatively, the rectangular enclosure might already have been heavily degraded by the time the hillfort was built. In its eroded state and distinctive shape we might then be seeing a glimpse of something altogether earlier, from the very start of the Iron Age, or even the preceding Bronze Age or Neolithic period. Air photography can suggest such possibilities; only excavation can prove or disprove them.

Cropmarks at Penygelli, near Newtown

Two very different cropmark enclosures stand on sloping ground above modern buildings. Here, the variation in size and shape might suggest a difference of function, like that between the farmhouse and stockyard in a present-day farm. Again, only excavation could reveal the true relationship.

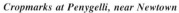

cluster round Roman forts, and perhaps belong to the Roman period? Can 'hybrid' shapes be identified, and if so did they develop in some way out of the simpler forms? Does the number of ditches at each site suggest variations in date or function, or simply indicate elaboration over time? Can different shapes, locations or complexities of 'defence' reveal gradations of power or social status? Do close neighbours, like those pictured on this page, really 'belong' with one another or are they simply using the same locality at widely differing dates?

Many of the cropmarks were mapped in the 1980s, for comparison with an area of lowland England in the Trent Valley. But it was not until 1990 that the Clwyd-Powys Archaeological Trust, long involved in air photography and excavation on the hillforts and small enclosures of the region, was able to begin a seven-year programme combining the continued mapping of air photographs with ground visits and, in due course, sample excavations to address some of the outstanding problems of dating, function and association.

From this combination of air survey, transcription, fieldwork and excavation quite a different picture of the Iron Age landscape is now beginning to emerge. The major forts remain unchanged, with perhaps varying functions as seats of power and centres of craft, trade and redistribution. They now sit, however, in a landscape which has a mass of smaller settlements on the hillslopes and lower ground. While some of these were perhaps minor seats of power, the majority were probably individual farmsteads or agricultural villages, related to each other

Borderland 'small enclosures' revealed as cropmarks
Scale 1:10,000. The largest enclosure measures just under 100 metres across.
(Examples taken from a report by the Clwyd-Powys Archaeological Trust.)

Hillforts and possibly Iron Age 'small enclosures' in the Upper Severn Valley
A *Major hillforts and other earthwork enclosures, mainly on higher land.*
B *The denser and more even distribution when cropmark sites are added.*
W, M, N = Welshpool, Montgomery, Newtown. Border marked by broken line.

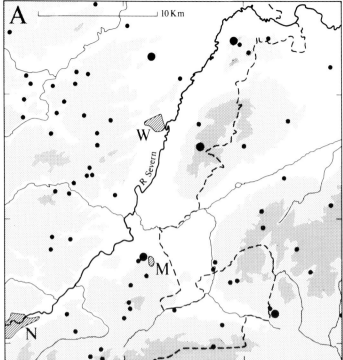

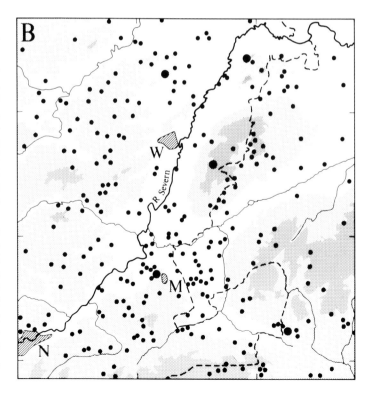

and to the larger forts in a fluctuating pattern of cooperation, conflict or dependency.

From excavation results we can reconstruct a partly wooded landscape, with extensive areas of managed pasture and arable cultivation around and between the settlements. Cattle and sheep were reared and pigs were eaten; wheat, barley and other crops were planted in the fields, and stored within the settlements. There was apparently a well-established system of trade, through exchange and barter rather than a money economy. Pottery and salt containers from the Malverns and Cheshire are found, for instance, on a variety of sites in the Upper Severn Valley during the later part of the period. Metalworking and other crafts may have been the prerogative of itinerant workers, or alternatively a household skill in all but the smallest settlements.

Compared with earlier views of warlike communities living largely on the hilltops, this radically changed picture is a striking testimony to the power of air photography to supplement the evidence of ground observation. But an unsettling corollary is that similar shortcomings in the basic data might apply to other parts of Wales, where air survey has yet to reach or where local conditions prevent the formation of cropmarks. In such areas we may be seeing too little of the settlement evidence for realistic analysis of the ancient landscape. More optimistically, perhaps, we should look forward to an intensified use of air photography, bringing similar transformations to other parts of Wales, where the ancient landscape may have a very different story to tell.

Camps, forts and roads of the Roman army

Air photography has played a critical role in uncovering the network of camps, forts and roads which mark the Roman domination of Wales from the first attacks in AD 48 until the middle of the second century. After that, the threat of danger in northern Britain became more pressing, and Wales was thought sufficiently pacified for many of the forts to be abandoned; in others the garrisons, and the forts themselves, were reduced in size.

From the air the traces of the Roman military mind are strikingly clear and consistent, the 'playing-card' outline of the forts and temporary camps contrasting starkly with the less precise shapes of earlier and later enclosures. The arrow-straight lines of the Roman roads, too, find few echoes in the more circuitous routes of later times.

Military works dominate this small group of pictures, but it must be remembered that the native population, however dominated by the Roman presence, continued to farm the land much as they did in earlier centuries. Now, however, as the money economy and trading patterns of the Roman world took hold, they had the responsibility or opportunity to supply the occupying troops and the craftsmen, traders and hangers-on who congregated in bustling civil settlements around most of the longer-lasting forts.

In the coming years air survey will continue to search for missing parts of the Roman military and road systems, and to seek traces of the half-glimpsed native communities who worked the Welsh landscape through the four centuries of Roman rule.

Roman marching camp at Esgairperfedd, Rhayader
The wavering lines of medieval and later trackways cut through the 'playing-card' shape of a temporary camp in the hill-country west of Rhayader.

Roman marching camps at Y Pigwn, between Brecon and Llandovery

Earthworks of this kind, supporting close-set palisades of stakes, could be thrown up in a matter of hours by the Roman troops for temporary protection. Here, deep in the central hills of Wales, successive campaigns in the first century AD are marked by overlapping camps, the larger for a force of around 10,000 men (up to two full legions), the smaller for perhaps half that number. The in-curving banks of protective 'claviculae' mark each of the entrances. The later Roman road from Brecon to Llandovery crosses the top of the picture, beneath modern tracks. Post-medieval tilestone quarries obscure the far side of the camps.

Roman fort at Caersŵs (left)

In this fine Cambridge University photograph, taken in early August 1976, the 'ghost' of the Roman fort surrounds farm buildings on the edge of the modern village. The typical playing-card shape is picked out by the darker marks of triple ditches, with a single-ditched annexe at the near end. The internal streets appear as lighter cropmarks, reflecting parching of the grass over the underlying stone foundations. Excavation evidence, from the middle of the nine-teenth century onwards, shows that the fort was founded in the mid-70s AD, almost certainly as the successor to an earlier fort sited on higher ground to the east (page 140). While the main period of military activity dates from the late first and early second centuries, at least some form of military or administrative presence continued into the third century, and perhaps even later. Beneath the modern village lies an extensive civil settlement associated with the fort, almost any modern disturbance producing Roman finds of one kind or another.

Castell Collen, Llandrindod Wells (right)

Above the steeply wooded bank of the River Ithon (top left) this finely preserved auxiliary fort still displays the traces of excavations which in 1911-13 uncovered the square headquarters building (centre) and a granary and 'barn' (left). The commandant's house lay in the confusion of trenches and spoil-tips to the right. The area beyond was taken up by timber barrack blocks for the 1000 or so troops garrisoned here from the late 70s AD. In the early third century the fort was reduced to an almost square shape, accommodating half the number of troops, by pulling back the defensive circuit from its earlier position in the foreground to a new line immediately in front of the excavated buildings. The garrison's bath-house, excavated in the 1950s along with three of the gates, lay outside the defences at top right, in a hollow just to the left of a single tree. Like many other Roman forts Castell Collen saw periods of abandonment and reoccupation during its long life, the final stage of renewal dating from the late third or early fourth century AD.

Cropmark fort at Llwyn-y-brain, Caersŵs

The Roman forts at Forden, south of Welshpool, and at Caersŵs, among the foothills of central Wales, were pivotal to the Roman hold on the mountainous regions, and continued in use long after most other forts had seen their garrisons withdrawn. At Caersŵs there were actually two forts, the later pictured on page 138. Here, the earlier fort is revealed in parched grassland during the summer drought of 1989, more than thirty years after its first discovery by Cambridge University air photographers.

Sited on raised land above the meanders of the River Severn, the fort occupies a stronger position than its successor, which stood on low ground beneath the modern village of Caersŵs (top), to protect river-crossings to its south and west. The earlier fort's triple ditches enclose an area about 220m by 170m across, large enough for a force of 1000 men or more. A fourth line of defence has an overlapping entrance in the foreground, a pattern seen elsewhere in campaign forts of the 50s AD. The fort's right-hand entrance is protected by a short extra length of ditch, or 'titulum', to deter a frontal attack on the gate. At the far end is a single-ditched annexe, perhaps for reinforcements or supplies when the troops moved further into the hills on campaign.

The Llwyn-y-brain fort probably went out of use when its successor was built in about AD 74-77.

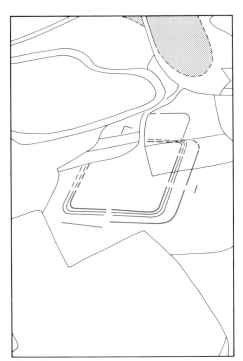

Roman marching camp, Nantmel, near Rhayader
This temporary camp near Rhayader, from one of the early Roman drives the hills of central Wales, was first identified by Dr A H A Hogg, former Secretary of the Royal Commission, while scanning Ordnance Survey 'vertical' photographs taken for mapping purposes in July 1971. Here it is seen in an 'oblique' view taken in low winter sunshine several years later, in November 1988.

Roman road near Llanerfyl, north of Caersŵs
One of best-preserved Roman roads in Wales runs north from the fort at Caersŵs towards the Banwy Valley and an unknown destination further north. In this view it strikes out across the moorland south of Llanerfyl, the alignment unbroken into the far distance. The curving section in the foreground shows that even Roman engineers had to adapt to the landscape, and in the middle distance the fairway makes a sharp detour to right and left in negotiating the sides of a deeply-cut stream bed. The sharp edges of the road reflect the stone-edged hardstanding on which it was laid in the late first or early second century AD.

Here, as elsewhere in Wales, the open moorland has been greened in recent years by reseeding for pasture improvement. While the first ploughing can throw slight earthworks of this kind into clear relief, each further ploughing to maintain this essentially artificial pasture cuts more deeply into the remains. Eventually they become so eroded that they are only visible as soilmarks after ploughing or as cropmarks in the parched grassland of the occasional summer drought.

'All the way from sea to sea'

*Rex nomine Offa qui vallum magnum inter Britanniam atque Merciam de
mari usque ad mare facere imperavit*
'A king named Offa who commanded a great bank to be built between
Britain [ie Wales] and Mercia all the way from sea to sea'

So wrote Bishop Asser at the end of the ninth century in his *Life of
Alfred*. On these few words hang the attribution to Offa, king of Mercia
from 757 to 796, of one of the most remarkable monuments in Britain, a
boundary work stretching nearly 200 kilometres from the Severn Estuary
near Chepstow to the Dee Estuary at Holywell, or even the North Wales
coast at Prestatyn (the route of the northernmost section is still in
dispute).

In the north, from the Upper Severn to Holywell, Offa's Dyke is
matched a little to the east by the scarcely less impressive Wat's Dyke. At
other places, especially to the west of Offa's Dyke in the central
Borderland, shorter dykes cut across ridge or valley routes used for
peaceable or warlike movement from pre-Roman times onwards.

It has been suggested that these 'short dykes' belong to the same
general scheme of boundary protection or regulation as Offa's Dyke, and
that Wat's Dyke represents an earlier attempt to secure Mercia's north-
western frontier during the forty-year reign of Offa's predecessor
Aethelbald. Alternative views see the short dykes as prehistoric, and
attribute Wat's Dyke to a later, rather than an earlier, episode of border
defence than Offa's great boundary work.

From the ground or from the air Offa's Dyke remains an enormously
impressive monument, striking boldly across the countryside, its bank
standing up to three metres high and its west-facing ditch often visible
despite centuries of erosion and re-filling. It is unclear, however, whether
the bank was ever crowned by a palisade or wall, or was permanently
manned except at narrow crossing points, none of which has yet been
identified with certainty. Moreover, there are substantial 'gaps' in its
course, notably in south Herefordshire. Some of these may represent
historical reality - where forest, marsh or river formed barrier enough, or
where local treaties made physical control unnecessary. Others may
simply reflect the ravages of time and the need for continuing fieldwork,
excavation and air photography to re-establish the line.

While uncertainties thus remain, the dykes themselves stand as
powerful reminders, both for the air photographer and for long-distance
walkers along the Offa's Dyke Path, of the struggle for control of the
Border country in the seventh to ninth centuries AD.

Offa's Dyke on the northern Borderland near Chirk
*In the summer view on the left the dyke runs south through the landscaped
parkland of Chirk Castle and into the distance as an unbroken line of trees. In
the winter view on the right, with the trees now stripped of their leaves, the
substantial scale of the bank can be appreciated as the dyke climbs onto higher
land south of the castle. At this point, as at many other places along its length,
the dyke still forms the boundary between England and Wales.*

'The palace in the lake'

Nineteenth-century finds of 'lake-dwellings' in Switzerland caused great excitement, and prompted exploration of many artificial islands, or 'crannogs', in Scotland and Ireland. Local antiquarians also dug into Ynys Bwlc, a small island in Llangors Lake, near the South Wales county town of Brecon.

The island proved indeed to be man-made, with layers of stone, soil and brushwood surrounded by two palisades of massive oak planks set upright into the floor of the lake. In the present century an Iron Age or Romano-British date was suggested for the crannog - one of only two yet known in Wales - after a dugout boat, supposedly of that period, was found nearby.

In the 1970s, however, the boat was re-dated by radiocarbon analysis to around the ninth century AD, and fresh attention was given to the island. Renewed exploration from 1987 has confirmed the earlier findings and shown that the D-shaped island was once linked by a raised walkway to the foreshore south of Llangors village, which had monastic connections in the tenth and earlier centuries. More critically, tree-ring dating of oak timbers fixed construction of the island firmly in the late ninth century AD. All now fell into place with a statement in the *Anglo-Saxon Chronicle* that in 916 'Aethelflaed sent an army into Wales and destroyed Brecenanmere and captured the king's wife and 33 other persons'. There can now be no doubt that the place attacked was the Llangors crannog, which was therefore a royal residence of Tewdwr ab Elisedd, king of Brycheiniog, the local Welsh kingdom of the time.

Finds of this or any other kind from the fifth to tenth centuries are so rare that the discovery assumes a special importance in the unfolding history of Wales, as will the continuing research on the island and the growing body of domestic debris and other finds recovered from the bed of the lake around it.

Dark Age crannog in Llangors Lake, near Brecon
Top. *The lake from the north-west, with the artificial island in the foreground.*
Above. *The island stands about forty metres offshore from the jetty on the north side of the lake.*
Right. *Excavation and survey work in progress in 1990 by teams from the National Museum of Wales and the University of Wales College of Cardiff.*

Castles of earth and timber

The kings of England, the Earls of Chester, Shrewsbury and Hereford and their followers, the marcher lords who succeeded them, the princes of Powys and of other Welsh territories, all these at one time or another competed for supremacy and created a society in which hostility and insecurity were features of everyday life. Castles large and small proliferated, sometimes of stone but more often of timber, a means both of defending land and property and extending their builders' authority into neighbouring areas.

So wrote Robert Higham and Philip Barker, speaking of the Borderland, in a recent book on timber castles. The authors emphasize that earth and timber castles were not just early or lowly versions of their masonry counterparts. In many cases they were royal or noble establishments, many of them occupied and some even built well into the thirteenth century, when stone castles were already common. In their heyday they were enormously imposing defences, their interiors heavily built up and thronging with activity. The main difference, for present-day appearances, lay in their more vulnerable building materials and the greater durability of castles built in stone.

Motte and bailey castle at Sycharth, Llansilin
One of the last-recorded motte and bailey castles to retain purely timber defences and buildings, Sycharth Castle, among the hills north of the Tanat Valley, so combined the needs of defence and a noble lifestyle that as late as about 1390 the travelling poet Iolo Goch sang lyrically of its dovecot, heronry and nine-roomed timber hall, along with the fish-ponds that can still be glimpsed at the very bottom of this view. Excavations in the 1960s confirmed that Iolo's hall sat on the summit of the motte, not in the lower bailey to the left. In 1403, barely twenty years after Iolo's visit, the castle and all its buildings were put to flames during the revolt of its owner, Owain Glyndŵr.

In all, Wales has over 300 earth and timber castles, about half of them along the Borderland - the densest concentration in Britain. They fall into three main types. **Ringworks** were strongly embanked and ditched enclosures, with timber gate towers and a variety of buildings in the interior. **Mottes** were deeply ditched or moated mounds, surmounted by a tall wooden tower within an imposing palisade and wall-walk; many, if not all, may have had palisaded outer enclosures or 'baileys' that do not survive above ground today. The third type, the **motte and bailey**, had at the base of the mound one or more embanked and ditched baileys, within which stood the castle's chapel, kitchen, barn, stables and the like.

Mottes were most commonly raised in the early years of Norman penetration, though geology or personal preference inspired the erection of ringworks in some areas. Over Wales as a whole, mottes - with or without surviving baileys - outnumber ringworks by about four to one. In the South East, however, ringworks predominate on the hard rocks of the 'Normanised' Vale of Glamorgan, while mottes outnumber them on the higher land to the north, where glacial moraines supplied ready-made mounds for adaptation.

Earthen castles were not entirely the work of the Norman invaders. On occasion the Welsh princes and princelings imitated the 'French' style of the incomers, with whom they fought and formed alliances in the two centuries before Wales finally succumbed to the dramatic stone castles of Edward I.

Ringwork at Waun Gunllwch, near Builth Wells
This fine ringwork south of Builth Wells occupies the end of a gently sloping promontory, above much steeper falls in the foreground. The massive circular ditch, with a bank on its outer lip, cuts off a defended platform about forty metres across. On the inner edge of the ditch a crescentic bank covers the promontory approach and causewayed entrance, but fades to almost nothing above the steep slopes on the near side of the castle. This effective but economical design, termed a 'partial ringwork', is common in topographical situations of this kind.

Castell Cymaron, near Llandrindod Wells
In hill-country north of Llandrindod Wells farm buildings occupy the bailey of an earth and timber castle of the Mortimer family, also known as Castell Cwm-Aran; a narrower outer bailey lies below and to the right. Overlooking the castle from higher ground to the left is a small mound, first noticed during aerial monitoring in 1986. Ground survey suggested that this was probably built as a siege-work for an undocumented attack on the castle. It is now legally protected, like the castle it once threatened to destroy.

Tomen Cefn-coch, Llanrhaeadr-ym-Mochnant
This simple motte west of the Tanat Valley is seven metres high, nearly forty metres across at the base and ten metres across at the top. The surrounding ditch is up to five metres wide and more than a metre deep on the uphill (far) side. No bailey is apparent on the ground, but appearances may be deceptive. From the air in times of drought there is a hint of a cropmark, perhaps representing the ditch of a ploughed-out bailey, extending from the mound towards the modern buildings in the foreground.

Builth Castle and the town of Builth Wells
Given scale by the streets and houses beyond, this motte and bailey castle looks down to the right over the river crossing which it was built to command. Founded by the Norman lord Philip de Braose in the 1090s, it changed hands between English and Welsh several times in the following century. Partially rebuilt in stone from the 1240s, it was entirely rebuilt by Edward I between 1277 and 1282. Now robbed of upstanding masonry, for rebuilding of the town after a disastrous fire near the end of the seventeenth century, it has returned to the form of its earth and timber origins. The motte, like many others in Wales, makes use of a natural eminence, adapted and enhanced by the builders in their castle construction. It was near Builth in December 1282 that Llywelyn ap Gruffydd ('Llywelyn the Last') met his death while seeking reinforcements for his struggle against Edward I.

Powis Castle: from timber castle to stately home

Visitors to Powis Castle, on the central Borderland at Welshpool, are attracted as much by the Italianate terraces and fine planting of its seventeenth-century gardens as by the grandeur of the stately home that it became from the sixteenth century onwards.

Documents record three early castles at Welshpool. One, the motte and bailey known as Domen Castell, overlooks the new bypass on the eastern fringes of the town. Another, Lady's Mount, stands in parkland beyond the castle, just out of sight in this view. The third, if the documents have been correctly interpreted, must have been Powis Castle itself. Whatever its original form, the castle had certainly begun to acquire stonework before the end of the thirteenth century under Owain de la Pole, the last of the native princes of Powys (and perhaps under his father too). Much of the medieval fabric survives, despite extensive alterations and additions in later periods.

Still the formal seat of the earl of Powis, the castle and its gardens are now owned by the National Trust.

Powis Castle, Welshpool

Vanishing traces of rural life

In comparison with the standing buildings of medieval and later years the more isolated or humble settlements of the Welsh countryside have been little studied. Certainly they are under-recorded from the air, though early photographs are now the best evidence we have for some of the settlements which have since been totally lost to ploughing for pasture improvement. In such cases the air photographs have become 'historic' documents in their own right, from which we must deduce what we can without benefit of surviving earthworks or walls.

The pictures on the next few pages are a reminder that many rural settlements, and some entire aspects of rural life such as rabbit farming, have all but vanished from the modern countryside, except for the meagre earthworks and as yet untapped documentary sources that survive for further study.

Every year, however, new areas of hillslope and upland pasture succumb to the plough, robbing us - eventually - of the farms, homesteads and enclosures that they once supported. In the coming years more attention needs to be turned to these vanishing traces of the ancient (and not so ancient) landscape. Our tools will not only be ground survey, excavation and documentary research, but also intensive programmes of exploration and recording from the air.

Pre-Norman fields at Hen Domen, Montgomery
Beyond the partly wooded oval the earth and timber castle built by Roger de Montgomery between about 1071 and 1086, evening shadows mark the slightly curving lines of ridge and furrow ploughing, a common agricultural pattern from the medieval period onwards. Here, however, excavation showed the ridges to continue under, and therefore to pre-date, the defensive bank of the castle. Barely perceptible on the ground, the ridges probably belong to Late Saxon cultivation of the rich lowland soil of this part of the Borderland. Their survival in a situation where a single ploughing could have destroyed them is a remarkable quirk of preservation.

Upland settlement, Cwm Berwyn, near Builth Wells
On a patch of unimproved pasture in the hills northeast of Builth Wells, a previously unrecorded settlement survives as a 'fan' of ridge and furrow cultivation, flanked by an embanked enclosure (perhaps an animal pound, at upper left) and the grassed-over foundations of a small rectangular 'long-hut'. Such settlements could date from any time in the twelfth to sixteenth centuries, or even later. In this case the irregularity of the ridges suggests that they may have been spade-dug rather than made by the plough.

Homestead and pillow mounds at Graig-fawr, near Llandrindod Wells

This fine Cambridge University photograph of 1969 is the best information we have for a medieval or post-medieval hut and attached enclosure in the central hills east of Llandrindod Wells. Narrow ridges below and to the right may represent spade-dug cultivation. In the next field to the right long, low 'pillow mounds' denote rabbit farming, a once-common land use which is also illustrated on page 152. Other mounds lie within the rampart of an Iron Age hillfort, which can just be glimpsed at extreme right. By 1977 modern ploughing had erased the cultivation ridges, and in 1981 there was nothing to be seen on the ground apart from a jumble of stones where the hut once stood. Even this has now almost vanished, though the pillow mounds still survive.

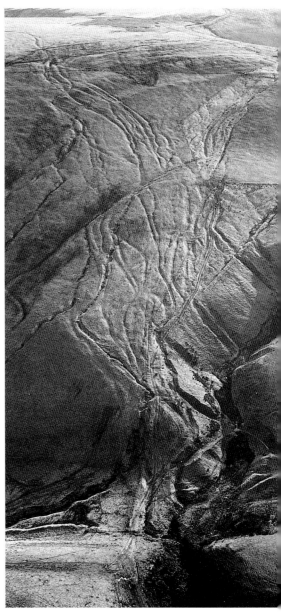

Long-distance trackways on Mynydd Cil-cwm
From the air, one of the most striking sights of Central Wales is the network of long-distance trackways that climb waveringly up from the valleys onto the less encumbered ridges and mountain plateaux. As each of these medieval or post-medieval trackways became too worn and muddy, a new line was sought alongside, eventually producing the 'braided' pattern seen here. This example lies deep in the heart of the Cambrian Mountains west of Newtown.

Upland settlements near Rhayader

Here, in the central uplands, three small settlements are seen in differing states of preservation.

At top left the earth and rubble banks of a small enclosure, originally square but now truncated by a modern fence and track, has a smaller and perhaps later enclosure within it and sits at the corner of an almost ploughed-out field or paddock, below and to the left.

In the foreground, in a small triangle of unimproved land immediately above the steep slopes of a stream gully, the well-preserved foundations of a rectangular hut and attached 'yard' perhaps belong to an abandoned summer steading or 'hafod'.

Finally, in heavily improved pasture on the right, an embanked enclosure, with a recessed 'platform-house' at its upper end, is so poorly preserved that it would surely not survive another ploughing.

All three settlements could be medieval or post-medieval in date. Even with close examination on the ground, however, it is probably too late to say whether they represent separate episodes, or a single scheme to exploit this seemingly inhospitable piece of upland pasture.

Ploughing and pillow mounds on Coed Swydd (left)
The farming of rabbits, for fur as well as flesh, was
part of the rural economy from at least the thirteenth
century until well into the nineteenth. Here, on an
isolated hilltop north-east of Pen-y-bont and Llandrindod Wells, two quite separate agricultural uses are
brought into focus by low winter sun and a light
dusting of snow. The long, low 'pillow mounds' of the
rabbit farm clearly overlie a finely preserved pattern
of earlier ridge and furrow ploughing. An embanked
enclosure in the background may belong to the rabbit
farm, or to a much earlier use of the hill in the pre-
Roman Iron Age. Pillow mounds also occur in a
number of other shapes, including simple round
mounds, as here. In essence they are artificial burrows,
often having stone-lined passageways and nesting
boxes within or beneath their earthen mounds.

The Brecon Forest Tramroad (right)
Superficially, the Brecon Forest tramroad looks like
an 'industrial' monument. It was first conceived,
however, as part of an ambitious plan to bring more
efficient farming to tracts of Fforest Fawr (the Great
Forest of Brecon) which were sold by the Crown to
help repay the debt created by the Napoleonic Wars.

   The purchaser, in 1820-22, was John Christie, a
rich and energetic London merchant, who quickly
established 'model' farms on his new estate. In order
to bring lime for soil improvement to these and other
farms in this wild upland landscape, Christie decided
to circumvent the rutted tracks of the local roads by a
carefully engineered and reliable horse-drawn tramroad, transporting lime directly from quarries or kilns
on his land.

   In the event, within six years the enterprise brought
Christie to financial ruin, not least through the
absence of the local coal reserves that had been
promised by the Crown Commissioners at the time of
the sale. Consequently, coal had to be brought uphill
before lime could be burnt on the mountain top. It is
the tramroad's southerly extension to the coalfield
that is pictured on the facing page, the sinuous course
of the contour-hugging tramroad contrasting with the
more direct route of the steam-powered Neath &
Brecon Railway of 1863-67.

   Despite Christie's personal failure, the relics of his
pioneering tramroad still find their place in the
landscape of the Brecon Forest. The history and
archaeology of the tramroad have been described in
one of the Royal Commission's published works,
listed on page 160.

Leighton Hall and its model farm

The Industrial Revolution was founded on the use of efficient means of production to create better goods and higher profits through economies of time, materials and labour.

By the middle of the nineteenth century there was a growing movement to apply similar ideas to farming. Stock was to be sheltered and better fed in winter, and manure was to be used with greater efficiency. Water and steam were to be harnessed for threshing and grinding, producing grain and flour for human consumption as well as fodder for the animals. Farm railways were even to be used for internal transport.

The capital for these improvements was available most readily on the large estates, and it was the renovation or replacement of their home farms that provided the 'model' farms for others to emulate.

The huge buildings of Leighton Hall Farm, on the Borderland near Welshpool, along with the estate's other buildings and its elaborate water and railway engineering, are arguably the most impressive surviving monument to these ideas in the United Kingdom. The farm buildings were laid out between 1848 and 1856 by the fabulously wealthy Liverpool banker, John Naylor, at a cost of £200,000. The vast scale of this investment may be judged by the fact that the whole estate had cost only £85,000 shortly before it was given to Naylor as a wedding present in June 1848.

Leighton Hall and its gardens, near Welshpool
The tall octagonal tower of Leighton Hall, built for John Naylor in 1850-56, forms a striking landmark in the Severn Valley near Welshpool. The now-decaying walled garden and greenhouses in the foreground were an essential part of any large estate well into the present century.

Leighton Home Farm, near Welshpool (right)
A broad-gauge railway traversed the three great barns that run diagonally down the centre of the picture and conveyed large loads of unthreshed corn to the turbine-powered thresher at the centre of the farm. Another single barn in line beyond the central thresher and machine-house probably stored the resultant straw. The fine circular sheds on the right, the nearer for pigs, the further for sheep, were late additions, along with the tall mill building which lies between them and the main complex.

Acknowledgements, equipment and sources of photographs

Acknowledgements

A book of this kind relies heavily on advice, comment and criticism from friends and colleagues, freely given and gratefully acknowledged. In addition to fellow staff in the Royal Commission, and former colleagues in the Welsh Archaeological Trusts, the author is indebted to Peter Crew, Dr Jeffrey Davies, Dr N J G Pearce and Dr Rowan Whimster for reading the whole or large parts of the text. Valued comments also came from Commissioners serving on the editorial, as listed on Contents page. Remaining faults are the author's alone.

The Royal Commission is grateful to the Clwyd-Powys, Dyfed and Gwynedd Archaeological Trusts for the use of photographs to fill gaps in its own collection. Cambridge University photographs, which add a significant 'historical' element, were provided through the good services of the current Curator in Aerial Photography, David R Wilson.

The author offers special thanks to the pilots whose skill and enthusiasm, given without thought of reward over many years, have contributed so much to Welsh air photography, and to this book in particular: Bob Jones, David Charles, John Small, Tony Joss, Tony Maitland, Jim Thomas, and especially Dr Ian Wallington, who first took the author into the air on a regular basis.

Royal Commission negatives were processed and printed by Fleur James and Iain Wright, who also took the photographs on page 30 and 26 respectively. All other photographs were taken by the author, apart from the excavation photograph on page 127 (Dr A M Gibson), the picture on page 58 (Terrence James) and those at the foot of page 81 and the top of page 89 (Richard Kelly). Prints from CPAT negatives were prepared by the author. The drawings are by Charles Green.

Photographic equipment and materials

All RCAHM and CPAT photographs were taken on Pentax 645 and Rollei 6002/6006 cameras, with 75mm, 80mm and 150mm lenses for black-and-white negatives and colour transparencies. Canon T70/T90 cameras were used for 35mm colour slides, with 50mm and 100mm FD lenses. Automatic exposures at 1/500 and 1/1000sec were provided by the cameras. Lens hoods and UV/Skylight filters were used in all cases, with 2x yellow filters for cropmark photography. Films were Kodak Tri-X (220), TMax 400, Fujichrome 100 and Kodachrome 200.

Sources of photographs

The page number, originating organization, reference number and date of each photograph is given below. Copyright rests with the named organizations, which should be contacted at the addresses shown below for prints or other reproductions.

RCAHM   Crown Copyright
Royal Commission on the Ancient and Historical Monuments of Wales, Crown Building, Plas Crug, Aberystwyth, SY23 1NJ.

CPAT   Clwyd-Powys Archaeological Trust, 7a Church Street, Welshpool, SY21 7DL.

CUCAP   Cambridge University Committee for Aerial Photography, Mond Building, Free School Lane, Cambridge, CB2 3RF.

DAT   Dyfed Archaeological Trust Ltd, The Shire Hall, Carmarthen Street, Llandeilo, SA19 6AF.

GAT   Gwynedd Archaeological Trust, Ffordd y Garth, Bangor, LL57 2SE.

Front cover: RCAHM, 945505-44, 01-05-94
Back cover: RCAHM, 94-CS-0206, 23-01-94
Title page, RCAHM, 93-CS-0106, 23-02-93
Contents page, CPAT, 79-1-31, 21-03-79
8 RCAHM, 90-CS-565, 19-07-90
10 RAF, 07-04-24; RCAHM copy, 915031-02
11 Top, CPAT, 86-MB-1205, 16-10-86
11 Bottom, CPAT, 88-16-23, 10-05-88
12 Top, CPAT, 87-C-199, 14-08-87
12 Middle, CPAT, 86-C-118, 29-07-86
12 Bottom, RCAHM, not numbered, 30-07-86
13 Top, RCAHM, 92-CS-0226, 26-06-92
13 Left, RCAHM, 90-CS-0509, 19-07-90
13 Centre, RCAHM, 90-CS-0562, 19-07-90
13 Right, RCAHM, 92-CS-0293, 27-01-92
14 Top, CPAT, 89-MB-1116, 29-07-89
14 Bottom, RCAHM, 945026-47, 23-01-94
15 Left, CPAT, 84-40-11, 26-12-84
15 Right, CPAT, 89-MB-1340, 08-08-89

15 Bottom, CPAT, 86-MB-473, 02-03-86
16 Left, RCAHM, 89-CS-0113, 09-05-89
16 Right, CPAT, 85-C-235, 23-07-85
18 CPAT, 84-MB-514, 22-07-84
21 RCAHM, 925501-06, 23-01-92
24 RCAHM, 94-CS-0588, 26-03-94
25 Top, RCAHM, 915514-15, 25-08-91
25 Bottom, RCAHM, 92-CS-0470, 02-07-92
26 RCAHM, 871500-14, 21-01-88
27 Top, RCAHM, 881713-18, 20-10-88
27 Left, RCAHM, 871538-21, 12-02-88
27 Right, RCAHM, 925024-28, 02-07-92
28 Left, RCAHM, 94-CS-0580, 26-03-94
28 Right, RCAHM, 945067-49, 24-03-94
29 Top left, RCAHM, 895502-17, 29-06-89
29 Top right, RCAHM, 905053-06, 01-08-90
29 Bottom left, RCAHM, 92-CS-0488, 02-07-92
29 Bottom right, RCAHM, 871537-07, 12-02-88
30 RCAHM, 905015-06, 24-05-90

31 Top, RCAHM, 945066-55, 24-03-94
31 Bottom, RCAHM, 945080-44, 26-03-94
32 Left, RCAHM, 92-CS-0465, 02-07-92
32 Right, RCAHM, 92-CS-0463, 02-07-92
33 Left, RCAHM, 871533-12, 12-02-88
33 Right, RCAHM, 895506-15, 04-04-89
34 CUCAP, BJP-69, 14-07-72
35 Top left, CUCAP, CBX-85, 04-03-77
35 Top right, CUCAP, FZ-15, 19-06-51
35 Bottom, CUCAP, FY-61, 19-06-51
36 Top, RCAHM, 94-CS-1222, 18-07-94
36 Bottom, RCAHM, 88-CS-0352, 07-12-88
37 Top, RCAHM, 945100-48, 18-04-94
37 Bottom, RCAHM, 925029-44, 30-07-92
38 Top, RCAHM, 905006-04, 26-03-90
38 Bottom, RCAHM, 925002-44, 31-01-92
39 Left, RCAHM, 925054-47, 19-10-92
39 Right, RCAHM, 905005-01, 26-03-90
40 RCAHM, 92-CS-1241, 21-10-92

41 RCAHM, 905540-18, 07-08-90
42 RCAHM, 881868-17, 28-10-88
43 RCAHM, 935047-63,19-03-93
44 RCAHM, 881440-02, 03-08-88
45 Bottom, RCAHM, 91-CS-0551, 26-08-91
45 Top, RCAHM, 94-CS-0627, 29-03-94
46 RCAHM, 915024-01, 25-08-91
47 RCAHM, 915024-07, 25-08-91
48 RCAHM, 93-CS-0246, 28-02-93
49 Top, CPAT, 87-C-149, 08-07-87
49 Bottom, RCAHM, 945099-44, 18-04-94
50 Top, RCAHM, 915013-18, 24-03-91
50 Bottom, RCAHM, 905045-17, 19-07-90
51 RCAHM, 905044-10, 19-07-90
52 RCAHM, 905521-12, 10-07-90
53 Top, RCAHM, 93-CS-0294, 28-02-93
53 Bottom, RCAHM, 935008-65, 23-02-93
54 Top, RCAHM, 905040-11, 19-07-90
54 Bottom, RCAHM, 905095-15, 15-12-90
55 RCAHM, 925010-58, 27-06-92
56 Top, RCAHM, 93-CS-0082, 23-02-93
56 Bottom, C R Musson, personal collection
57 Top, RCAHM, 93-CS-0087, 23-02-93
57 Bottom, C R Musson, personal collection
58 DAT (T A James), AP85-94.30, 01-06-85
59 RCAHM, 925020-41, 02-07-92
60 Top, RCAHM, 935023-55, 02-07-93
60 Bottom, RCAHM, 945051-45, 15-03-94
61 RCAHM, 905518-02, 18-07-90
62 RCAHM, 895020-09, 18-05-89
63 RCAHM, 905086-10, 14-12-90
64 Left, RCAHM, 89-CS-0153, 18-05-89
64 Right, RCAHM, 905546-03, 14-12-90
65 Left, CUCAP, CY-44, 17-06-49
65 Right, RCAHM, 93-CS-0661, 01-04-93
66 RCAHM, 925008-67, 27-06-92
67 RCAHM, 905077-01, 27-09-90
68 Top, RCAHM, 93-CS-0664, 01-04-93
68 Bottom, RCAHM, 935023-47, 23-02-93
69 Top, RCAHM, 91-CS-0281, 24-03-91
69 Bottom, RCAHM, 90-CS-0928, 27-09-90
70 Top, RCAHM, 915015-25, 24-03-91
70 Bottom, RCAHM, 915015-10, 24-03-91
71 RCAHM, 935032-41, 27-02-93
72 Left, RCAHM, 89-CS-0021, 25-04-89
72 Right, RCAHM, 89-CS-0079, 25-04-89
73 Top, RCAHM, 92-CS-1283, 29-10-92
73 Bottom, RCAHM, 92-CS-1387, 20-10-92
74 Left, RCAHM, 935041-49, 28-02-93
74 Right, RCAHM, 895019-19, 18-05-89
75 RCAHM, 905078-03, 27-09-90
76 RCAHM, 93-CS-1168, 04-05-93
77 Top, RCAHM, 89-CS-0623, 11-07-89
77 Bottom, RCAHM, 905514-05, 03-07-90
78 CUCAP, ABQ-30, 29-06-60
80 RCAHM, 905515-11, 03-07-90

81 Top, RCAHM, 915503-03, 26-02-91
81 Bottom, GAT, 2798.3, 26-11-87
82 Top, RCAHMW, 945134-53, 30-05-94
82 Bottom, CUCAP, AKX-2, 20-05-65
83 RCAHM, 935112-61, 04-05-93
84 RCAHM, 935506-15, 04-05-93
85 RCAHM, 935506-02, 04-05-93
86 RCAHM, 945094-53, 17-04-94
87 RCAHM, 945119-54, 01-05-94
88 RCAHM, 93-CS-1139, 04-05-93
89 Top, GAT, 2132.9, 12-04-90
89 Bottom, RCAHM, 94-CS-0969, 01-05-94
91 RCAHM, 935117-55, 04-05-93
92 Top, RCAHM, 94-CS-0738, 17-04-94
92 Left, RCAHM, 94-CS-0915, 01-05-94
92 Right, RCAHM, 935064-61, 25-03-93
93 RCAHM, 94-CS-0942, 01-05-94
94 CUCAP, BQ-2, 20-07-48
95 CPAT, 90-MB-510, 04-04-90
96 Left, RCAHM, 93-CS-1125, 04-05-93
96 Right, RCAHM, 93-CS-1098, 04-05-93
97 Top, RCAHM, 93-CS-1101, 04-05-93
97 Bottom, RCAHM, 93-CS-1104, 04-05-93
98 Top, RCAHM, 895036-18, 11-07-89
98 Bottom, RCAHM, 945144-67, 30-05-94
99 RCAHM, 895036-12, 11-07-89
100 RCAHM, 905522-08, 11-07-90
101 Top, CPAT, 84-C-58, 26-06-84
101 Bottom, CPAT, 85-C-324, 23-07-85
102 Top, RCAHM, 945111-50, 30-04-94
102 Bottom, RCAHM, 935138-54, 23-06-93
103 RCAHM, 935134-43, 21-05-93
104 RCAHM, 895502-04, 26-06-89
105 Top, RCAHM, 945110-51, 30-04-94
105 Bottom, CPAT, 87-MB-999, 13-08-87
106 CUCAP, AWP-41, 27-01-69
107 CUCAP, K17-AI-186, 07-07-75
108 CPAT, 89-C-190, 26-06-89
109 CPAT, 84-C-245, 19-07-84
110 RCAHM, 915005-10, 26-02-91
111 CPAT, 84-MB-295, 19-07-84
112 Top, RCAHM, 89-CS-0634, 11-07-89
112 Bottom, CPAT, 86-C-100, 21-07-86
113 Top, CPAT, 88-MC2-14, 05-05-88
113 Bottom, RCAHM, 93-CS-0725, 04-04-93
114 Top, RCAHMW, 905033-13, 11-07-90
114 Bottom, RCAHM, 935086-47, 04-04-93
115 RCAHM, 905030-05, 11-07-90
116 Top, CPAT, 85-C-191, 21-07-85
116 Bottom, CPAT, 84-C-61, 26-06-84
117 CPAT, 89-MB-209, 11-03-89
118 Top, CPAT, 89-MB-206, 11-03-89
118 Left, CPAT, 89-MB-226, 11-03-89
118 Right, CPAT, 89-MB-204, 11-03-89
119 RCAHM, 935136-49, 21-05-93
120 Top, RCAHM, 90-CS-0517, 11-07-90

120 Bottom, CPAT, 84-19-8, 13-05-84
121 RCAHM, 905522-12, 11-07-90
122 Top, CPAT, 86-MB-492, 02-03-86
122 Bottom, CPAT, 86-MB-498, 02-03-86
123 CPAT, 86-MB-505, 02-03-86
124 CPAT, 85-C-263, 23-07-85
125 Top, RCAHM, 905511-12, 24-05-90
125 Bottom, RCAHM, 905510-14, 24-05-90
126 Left, CUCAP, AYT-46, 13-07-69
126 Right, CUCAP, BUH-11, 12-07-75
127 Top, CPAT, excavation archive
127 Bottom, RCAHM, 915003-09, 26-02-91
128 Top, CPAT, 84-MB-516, 22-07-84
128 Centre, CPAT, 86-MB-915, 26-07-86
128 Bottom, CPAT, 84-C-337, 22-07-84
129 Top, RCAHM, 92-CS-113, 19-10-92
129 Bottom, RCAHM, 92-CS-0514, 06-07-92
130 Top, RCAHM, 945028-46, 23-01-94
130 Bottom, CPAT, 83-15-28, 05-08-83
131 Top, RCAHM, 935092-53, 12-04-93
131 Bottom, RCAHM, 925092-48, 08-12-92
132 Top, CPAT, 84-C-164, 07-07-84
132 Left, CPAT, 80-C-286, 12-11-80
132 Right, CPAT, excavation archive, 1982
133 RCAHM, 895508-04, 08-08-89
134 Top, CPAT, 89-MB-613, 24-089
134 CPAT, 79-12-20, 26-07-79
136 CPAT, 88-C-104, 21-11-88
137 RCAHM, 925502-12, 27-01-92
138 CUCAP, CAZ-17, 04-08-76
139 RCAHM, 945071-60, 26-03-94
140 RCAHM, 895509-05, 08-08-89
141 Left, CPAT, 88-MB-601, 21-11-88
141 Right, RCAHM, 93-CS-0956, 04-05-93
142 RCAHM, 935138-42, 23-06-93
143 RCAHM, 945023-41, 23-01-94
144 Top, RCAHM, 92-CS-0499, 06-07-92 ^KG
144 Left, RCAHM, 90-CS-0540, 12-07-90
144 Right, RCAHM, 90-CS-0542, 12-07-90
145 RCAHM, 93-CS-0679, 04-04-93
146 Top, CPAT, 87-MB-251, 19-04-87
146 Bottom, CPAT, 86-MB-1184, 16-10-86
147 Left, RCAHM, 935097-47, 02-05-93
147 Right, RCAHM, 925066-44, 29-10-92
148 RCAHM, 905504-13, 04-04-90
149 Top, CPAT, 84-41-7, 26-12-84
149 Bottom, RCAHM, 88-CS-0145, 02-08-88
150 CUCAP, AZW-78, 05-11-69
151 Left, RCAHM, 925086-45, 08-12-92
151 Right, RCAHM, 925096-45, 20-12-92
152 RCAHM, 92-CS-0071, 11-01-92
153 RCAHM, 881864-07, 28-10-88
154 RCAHM, 905076-17, 14-09-90
155 RCAHM, 905076-11, 14-09-90
160 RCAHM, 93-CS-0658, 01-04-93

Index to illustrated sites

Further reading.............see also next page

A History of Wales, by John Davies, Allen Lane/Penguin, 1993.

Settlement and Society in Wales, edited by D Huw Owen, University of Wales, 1989.

The Historic Architecture of Wales: An Introduction, by John B Hilling, University of Wales, 1976.

Air Photo Interpretation for Archaeologists, by D R Wilson, Batsford, 1982.

The Emerging Past, by Rowan Whimster, Royal Commission on the Historical Monuments of England, 1989. Analysis and mapping of cropmark evidence.

History from the Air, by Richard Muir, Michael Joseph, 1983.

'Cambridge Air Surveys', published by the Cambridge University Press:
  Roman Britain from the Air, by S S Frere and J K S St Joseph, 1983.
  Castles from the Air, by R Alan Brown, 1989.
  Industrial history from the air, by Kenneth Hudson, 1984.

The Oxford Illustrated Prehistory of Europe, edited by Barry Cunliffe, Oxford University, 1994.

Prehistoric Britain, by Timothy Darvill, Batsford, 1987.

Bronze Age Britain, by Michael Parker Pearson, Batsford, 1993.

Iron Age Communities in Britain, by Barry Cunliffe, Routledge, 1991.

The Oxford Illustrated History of Roman Britain, by Peter Salway, Oxford University, 1993.

Britannia: a history of Roman Britain, by Sheppard Frere, Routledge, 1987. Also available as Pimlico paperback.

The Roman Frontier in Wales, by V E Nash-Williams, revised by Michael G Jarrett, University of Wales, 1969.

Wales in the Early Middle Ages, by Wendy Davies, Leicester University, 1982.

Early Medieval Settlements in Wales, AD 400-1100, edited by Nancy Edwards and Alan Lane, University of Wales, 1988.

Offa's Dyke, by Sir Cyril Fox, British Academy, 1955.

Timber Castles, by Robert Higham and Philip Barker, Batsford, 1992.

Castles in Wales and the Marches, edited by John R Kenyon and Richard Avent, University of Wales, 1987.

The King's Works in Wales, 1277-1330, by A J Taylor, HMSO, 1974.

Castles in Wales, by Roger Thomas, AA/Wales Tourist Board, 1988.

Castles of the Princes of Gwynedd, by Richard Avent, HMSO, 1983.

Medieval Monasteries, by J Patrick Greene, Leicester University, 1922.

The Towns of Medieval Wales, by Ian Soulsby, Phillimore, 1983.

The Historic Gardens of Wales, by Elisabeth Whittle, HMSO, 1992.

The Industrial Archaeology of Wales, by D Morgan Rees, David & Charles, 1975.

Welsh Industrial Heritage, a review, edited by C Stephen Briggs, Council for British Archaeology, 1992.

Welsh Coal Mines, by W Gerwyn Thomas, and **Welsh Industrial Workers Housing 1775-1875**, by J B Lowe, National Museum of Wales, 1986, 1977.

History of the North Wales Slate Industry, by Jean Lindsay, David & Charles, 1974.

Cardiff and the Valleys, by John B Hilling, Lund Humphries, 1973.

A Guide to Ancient and Historic Wales, regional guides by HMSO for Cadw:Welsh Historic Monuments. 'Glamorgan and Gwent', by Elisabeth Whittle, and 'Dyfed', by Siân Rees, both 1992; others to follow.

Cadw's 56-page **Guides** to abbeys, castles and other monuments in their care provide excellent introductions to the sites and their historical background.

Royal Commission publications

Enquiries to the Royal Commission,
Crown Building, Plas Crug,
Aberystwyth, SY23 1NJ

Houses of the Welsh Countryside: A Study in Historical Geography, 2nd edition
By Peter Smith

Inventory volumes still available for Glamorgan and Brecknock
Glamorgan The Early Castles
Medieval Secular Monuments: Non-defensive
The Greater Houses
Farmhouses and Cottages
Brecknock   The Prehistoric and Roman Monuments, Part II, Hill-forts and Roman Remains

Llantwit Major and Cowbridge: A Study of the Historic Domestic Architecture

Newport Castle (Pembrokeshire): An Architectural Study, by David M Browne and David Percival

From Alan Sutton Publishing,
Phoenix Mill, Far Thrupp,
Stroud, Gloucs, GL5 2BU

The Archaeology of the Montgomeryshire Canal: A Guide and Study in Waterways Archaeology
By Stephen Hughes

A Guide to the Industrial Archaeology of the Swansea Region, 2nd edition
By Stephen Hughes and Paul Reynolds

The Archaeology of an Early Railway System: The Brecon Forest Tramroads
By Stephen Hughes

Lighthouses of Wales, Their Architecture and Archaeology
By D B Hague (edited by Stephen Hughes)

Collieries of Wales, Their Architecture and Engineering
By Stephen Hughes, Brian Malaws, Medwyn Parry and Peter Wakelin

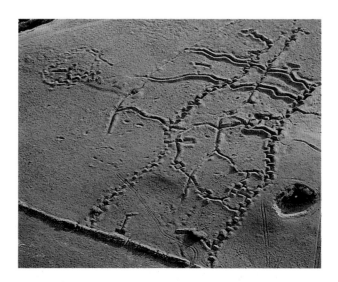

Practice trenches from World War I
Penally, near Tenby, Pembrokeshire